DESERTED
SCHOOLHOUSES
OF IRELAND

Enda O'Flaherty is an archaeologist based in Ireland with a particular interest in vernacular architecture and the buildings and landscape of rural Ireland. He is the founder of the Disused Schoolhouses blog (endaoflaherty.com), and has spent over a decade and a half working as an archaeologist in Ireland and abroad, studying the remains of settlements from both the recent and distant past. His explorations of Ireland as a wandering archaeologist gave him a wish to understand better the deep and defining importance of the interaction between people and landscape. He now focuses on more recent remains of the past, and is undertaking a PhD at NUI Galway, examining human settlement in karst landscapes. He lives in Cork.

DESERTED

SCHOOLHOUSES

OF IRELAND

Enda O'Flaherty

The Collins Press

First published in 2018 by
The Collins Press
West Link Park
Doughcloyne
Wilton
Cork
T12 N5EF
Ireland

A CIP record for this book is available from the British Library.

Hardback ISBN: 978-1-84889-351-1

Design and typesetting by Anú Design, Tara
Typeset in Adobe Caslon
Printed in Poland by Białostockie Zakłady Graficzne SA

Cover photographs
Front: Bunglash National School, County Kerry; *spine*: Shanvaghera National School, County Mayo; *back* (clockwise from top): Latton National School, County Monaghan; Bunnanadden National School, County Sligo; Shanvaghera National School, County Mayo. (All photographs by Enda O'Flaherty)

To Emmet

Some of the schoolhouses featured in this book lie in the middle of agricultural fields, or on private lands, without a public pathway that provides easy access. Readers of this book should note that this publication is an information guide and does not act as an invitation to enter any of the properties or sites listed. Often, these buildings are in private ownership and consent to access the buildings must be sought before entering. No responsibility is accepted by the author or publisher for any loss, injury or inconvenience sustained by anyone as a result of using this book.

If you or someone you know attended any of the national schools featured in this book, please get in touch and share any stories, anecdotes, photographs, or any other memories you may have. Visit: www.endaoflaherty.com

Contents

Acknowledgements

A sincere thank-you to all who have supported the disused schoolhouses project and this publication. Special thanks to all those who contributed their memories and thoughts over the past few years, and everyone I've chatted to on roadsides since 2014. Your support and encouragement meant the world to me. I'll do my best to remember everyone: Joe Callan, Kathleen and James McTague, Joanne Curnan and the Corraleehan Historical and Cultural Society, Myra Reynolds, Pat Mulreany, Damien Shiels and the staff at Rubicon Heritage, P.J. Curtis, Lynda McCormack and the Institute of Archaeologists of Ireland, Mark Oldham, Petra Blomberg, all at The Collins Press, Máirín Uí Fhearraigh, Sonia Nic Giolla Easbuig, Amanda Clarke, Síle Uí Ghallchóir, Mary Galligan, Tanya O'Halloran, Anne Mc Cann, Bill L. Wood, Catherine Molloy-Leavy, Carla Kirby, Joseph Tyrrell, Philip Butler, Teresa Reichenbach Parlette, Noah Dixon, Christopher Wayne, Rory McGinley, Dee Halloran, Simon Linnell, Ginger Aarons, Harry Reid, Sinead Boland, Lynda Cronin, Margaret O'Driscoll, Tony P. Quinn, Brian Ellis, Jay Henry, Jörgen Hartogs, Caroline Horan, Noelle Callaghan, Angela Power, Eva Ní Shuilleabháin, Greg Hayes, Kieran Ring, Orla Peach-Power and the Virtual Heritage Network, Heritage Week Ireland, Anne Petrie, Kris Hirst, David Cowhey, Bernie Carney, Tony and the Mixed Messages Blog, Angela Gallagher, Jason Fallon, Pete McCarthy, Laurence Jones, Roscommon Town History & Heritage, Caoimhe Cronin and Dougal, Ian Russell, Donie Brady, Bernie McGovern, Vicky Droll, Patricia Higgins, David Donovan, Jean Schneider, Dennis Burke, Genie McGuire, Anika Burgess and Atlas Obscura, Mary Galligan, Geraldine Greene, Brigid Barry, Bernice Kelly, Noreen O'Rinn, Sean Nolan and *Ireland's Own*, Kathryn Chou, Jerome Kelly, Bob Howley, Max Chevers, Laurence Jones, Patrick Balester, Paddy Kilbane.

A view through a broken window
into Tullaghan National School in
County Leitrim.

Introduction

In early 2014 I started casually photographing abandoned schoolhouses around Ireland. I don't have one true explanation for why I began: this hobby started by accident and had no real projected outcome. Over the following months and years, I uploaded my snaps to an online blog and from there a project to document and explore the disused schoolhouses of the rural Irish landscape developed. Between 2014 and 2017 I visited and photographed about 240 abandoned schoolhouses, talking to people who had attended the schools, and exploring the historical background of each one. Every empty building had a story to tell, and collectively they whispered a sometimes underappreciated and unrecognised narrative about a changing modern Ireland and rural decline in the latter part of the twentieth century. The result of this work is this publication.

There is little or no previous research that examines the historical and contemporary social and cultural significance of early rural schoolhouses in Ireland. The physical remains of only some of these institutional buildings had been recorded in the National Inventory of Architectural Heritage (NIAH) of Ireland (1990 to the present), and the buildings were afforded varying degrees of protection on architectural merit alone. The schoolhouses were neglected and collapsing. Each weekend I would travel to some far-flung part of the country to photograph these forgotten buildings. The photographs revealed the ruinous physical environment and prompted locals to come forward and share what they remembered about the local schoolhouse. Many had been shut down through the latter half of the twentieth century and reflected the decline in the local rural population. From the northern borderlands to the offshore islands, and from west Donegal to the peninsulas of west Cork and Kerry, the story was one of emigration and decline. Weather-beaten and collapsing, these schoolhouses were the withering fruit on the dying vine of rural life.

The schoolhouse as a heritage object is a common symbol of a shared past within both local communities and the wider population. It was a shared space recognised and remembered by all within a community through multiple

Latton National School, County Monaghan – built in 1941, now empty and exposed to the elements. A new modern national school has been built nearby.

generations. It was a place full of memory and meaning for those who still lived nearby, and those who had left.

Aside from an individual's family, few things have greater impact on our development and personality, our understanding of the world around us and the mechanisms we use to deal with and interpret that world than our experience of the classroom and schoolyard. In exploring and photographing these crumbling buildings, I was also walking through countless childhoods and earliest memories.

Today, you will generally find these empty buildings in the most sparsely populated of areas. Often hidden on mountainsides or crumbling behind ivy, they remain as testament to times past, and symbols of a changed way of life in rural Ireland. These are now ruinous spaces. And contemporary ruins can provoke an unusual emotional response that is difficult to define.

Decaying buildings signify the inevitable process of history to which we all will eventually succumb, a kind of time travel to the future within the past. The

DESERTED SCHOOLHOUSES OF IRELAND

schoolhouse was an environment with powerful emotional connections: school was where you met your friends and built bonds that often lasted a lifetime. Every corner of these buildings I photographed would still be familiar to past pupils.

However, the now-empty buildings are a potent reminder of rural Ireland's long tradition of emigration. For many who emigrated at an early age, their days spent in these rural and isolated schoolhouses were often the last formal education they received before seeking a brighter future abroad. Although many of these buildings are now physically empty or approaching a point of collapse,

Laughil National School, Rabbitpark townland, County Longford. It was built in 1937 to replace an earlier building. The surrounding landscape is rural and empty, though a schoolhouse has been located here since the 1840s.

the physical structures hold a wealth of memory and associations. From these small rural schoolhouses many children took what they had learned and went out to find fortune and to explore the greater world.

Although the written history of education and the architecture preserved in schoolhouses presents one facet of their historical significance, it is the emotional connection with 'place' that draws out the personal narratives of what it was like to attend school in one of these buildings. This, to me, is the most valuable and least appreciated significance of these deserted schoolhouses, and it is what I hope to show in the pages that follow.

Although the schoolhouse reflected different values and experiences for different people, it was still a common symbol of a shared past. It was a shared space that was recognised and remembered by all within a community through multiple generations. It was a place full of memory and meaning for those who still lived nearby, and those who had left.

A brief history of the schoolhouse and education in Ireland

To begin our exploration of the decaying and abandoned schoolhouses of Ireland, it might be a good idea to take a quick look at the origins of these buildings, the historical background to their establishment and the ideology behind education in Ireland from the beginning of the nineteenth century onward. Also important is an explanation of why there are so many schoolhouses scattered across the landscape, particularly in the most rural parts of Ireland.

The history of education in Ireland has previously been the subject of comprehensive study; however, the physical environment and architectural surroundings of nineteenth- and early-twentieth-century schoolhouses has only occasionally received dedicated, region-specific study. Many of the school buildings featured in this book are considered unimportant from an architectural perspective, and so this publication is perhaps the first examination of the generic rural schoolhouse in Ireland.

By generic rural schoolhouse, I am referring to the early one- and two-room rural schoolhouses constructed from the early to mid nineteenth century onwards. Some were elaborate Victorian or Edwardian constructions with cut-stone facades, beautiful sash windows and intricate wrought-iron metal work, and many of these still stand and function today. But many more were simple

The date plaque on Auchaconey National School in Aghaconny, County Cavan, showing it to have been built in 1886.

Sonnagh National School in the Slieve Aughty Mountains, County Galway. This typical one-room schoolhouse was built in 1891 to one of the standard plans supplied by the Office of Public Works. Its form is basic and its architecture functional at best. Once a thriving rural community, the former farmlands that surrounded the school are now planted with commercial forestry and very few people live in the area today.

What remains of
the outdoor toilets
to the rear of
Willbrook National
School, Craggaunboy
townland in
County Clare.

buildings erected particularly in the latter half of the nineteenth century, and built to a number of specific designs supplied by the Office of Public Works (OPW). It is these 'to-plan' buildings that are the most overlooked. We will take a look at why this is the case a little later on.

A definition of a one-room schoolhouse is a school consisting of one classroom where a single teacher taught academic basics to several grade levels of elementary-age boys and girls. The one-room schoolhouse is to be found in many countries both in Europe and overseas, but is characteristic of rural areas with sparse populations, for example Ireland, Shetland, New Zealand, Scandinavia, Canada and Australia. Although many one-room schoolhouses were built, small two-room schoolhouses were also constructed where required, usually with boys and girls being taught in separate classrooms. These were simple buildings comprising an entrance hall, classroom and surrounding yard with outdoor toilets, usually to the rear. In Ireland, you can find these now often abandoned buildings wherever there has been a decline in population, where rural life has changed, where once-bustling market towns have become ghost towns with boarded-up shopfronts under faded family names, and where the traditional small farmsteads have been consolidated or abandoned. The one-room schoolhouse is symbol of another time and a fading past.

Prior to the early nineteenth century, formal education in Ireland was primarily a privilege for the elite, non-Catholic classes. This was particularly true during the eighteenth century when Catholics were forbidden to be educated under the Penal Laws from 1695 to 1782. Catholic children were educated by means of the somewhat secretive and unofficial 'hedge schools', usually taught by an educated person from the locality or a travelling schoolmaster. 'Hedge school' was the name given to this educational practice because of its rural nature rather than the schooling being held outdoors. However, Arthur Young, travelling in Ireland in the 1770s, claimed that the most appropriate name for them would be 'ditch schools', for he had seen many 'ditches full of scholars'[2]. The tradition of building the school by a ditch was known before the Penal Laws, however, as shown in this example during the reign of Charles II: 'Stephen Gelosse, S.J. has been working in and near New Ross this year 1669, and ever since 1650 … When Cromwell's tyranny ceased, Father Gelosse … taught a small school … in a wretched hovel beside a deep ditch, and there educated a few children furtively'.[3]

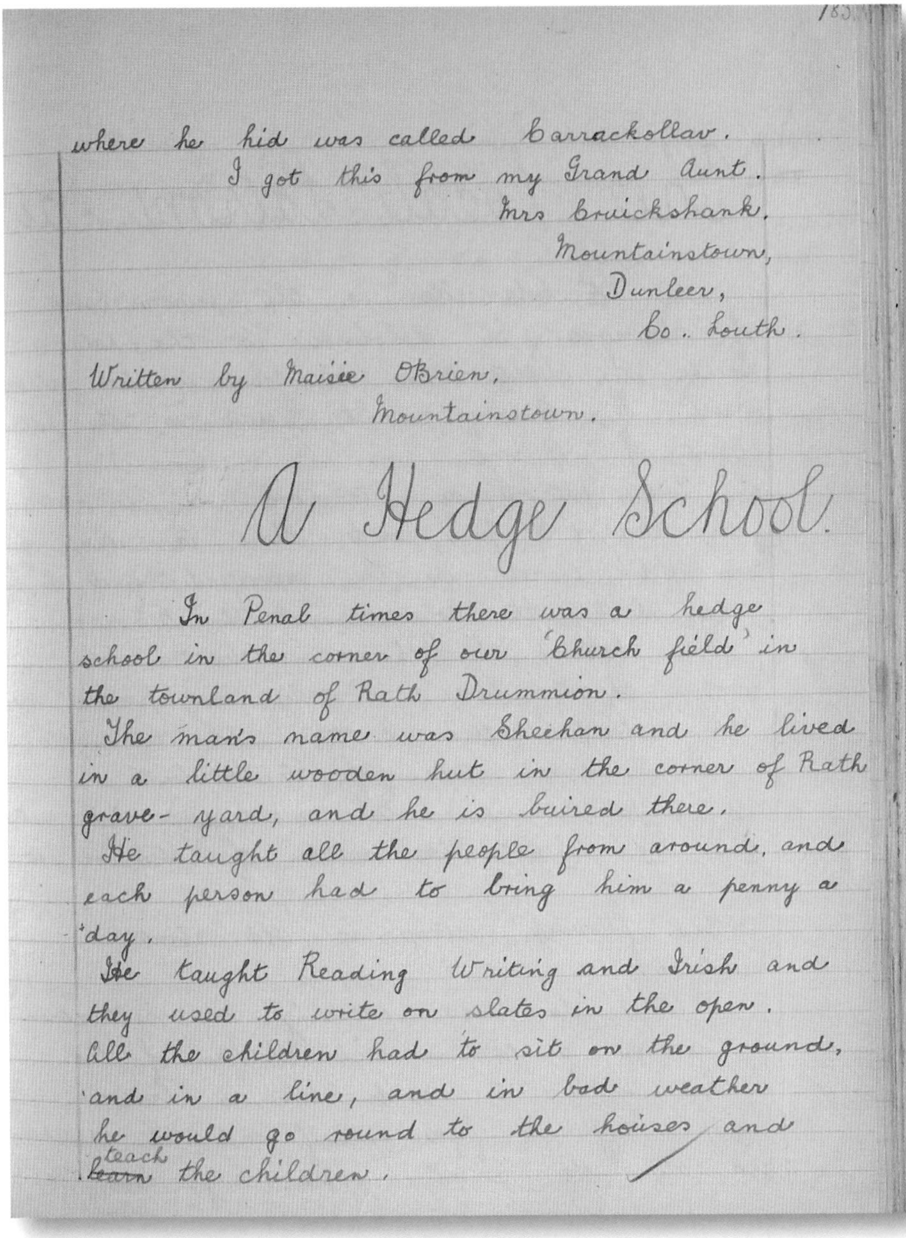

where he hid was called Carrackollav.

I got this from my Grand Aunt.

Mrs Cruickshank,

Mountainstown,

Dunleer,

Co. Louth.

Written by Maisie OBrien,

Mountainstown.

A Hedge School.

In Penal times there was a hedge school in the corner of our 'Church field' in the townland of Rath Drummion.

The man's name was Sheehan and he lived in a little wooden hut in the corner of Rath grave-yard, and he is buired there.

He taught all the people from around, and each person had to bring him a penny a day.

He taught Reading Writing and Irish and they used to write on slates in the open.

All the children had to sit on the ground, and in a line, and in bad weather he would go round to the houses and teach the children.

An extract from the Schools Folklore Commission Records for Díseart, Droichead Átha (Dysart County Louth: Roll Number 1434) describing a local hedge school that operated in the locality prior to the construction of a schoolhouse there in 1835.

In the eighteenth and early nineteenth centuries, education was one of the great bones of contention between the Catholic Church and the government, and the alleged disabilities of Catholics with regard to education was an important plank in nationalist propaganda.[4] Through the course of the eighteenth century many working people of a non-Catholic background learned to read, and the desire for some literacy grew. This desire was widespread in the towns on the east coast of Ireland, but was reportedly virtually non-existent among the Gaelic-speaking cottiers on the west coast. Outside of the clandestine hedge-school system for Catholic children, anyone, even with the most limited education themselves, could start a school in even the most unsuitable buildings. These could be barns, or rented rooms or tiny church halls.

A view inside the classroom of Kilnaboy National School, County Clare. The schoolhouse was built on land donated by a local family in 1884. A teacher's desk stands in the centre of the photograph.

To formalise the education system to some degree, in 1806 the Irish Chancellor of the Exchequer, Sir John Newport, persuaded the Lord Lieutenant the Duke of Bedford to set up an inquiry on the spending of public money on education. The commission produced several reports, but the last report in 1812 would be by far the most important. It concluded that the only option to educate the population while pleasing every religious denomination would be a neutral, mixed, national system.

The Kildare Place Society had already been formed in 1811 explicitly to cater for the demand for education among the Catholic poor, and aimed to provide a Bible-based but non-denominational education that would be acceptable to Catholics. However, it was also to establish schools that would subsequently be managed on the principles of the 1812 report, to provide the buildings, supply the books and other school necessities cheaply, and to train teachers. In 1816 the society petitioned Parliament and was awarded £10,000, an amount that was greatly increased over the following decade; this money allowed it to spread across the country and to establish the rudiments of a national system of primary education. Despite some straying in the direction of a biblical education, it would seem that the gentlemen of the Kildare Place Society were the only group in Ireland in the whole of the nineteenth century (apart from the gentlemen on the National Board) who were genuinely interested in education. The Catholic clergy especially realised that they could not compete, school for school, with the government-assisted and allegedly proselytising Kildare Place Society. At the request of the Catholic Bishops another commission on education was established, and it recommended the formation by the government of a national school board, which would take over the functions and duties of the Kildare Place Society and receive its grant. However, the Society continued its work, albeit on a reduced scale, to the end of the century.

The aforementioned hedge schools became legal when Catholic Emancipation was achieved in 1829 (Roman Catholic Relief Act 1829); however, the national system of education introduced in Ireland in 1831 formalised the process of education and, importantly, introduced financial incentives and assistance to local communities for the construction of new schoolhouses. Lacking official status, hedge schools were considered part of the informal education sector. Certainly, the introduction of national schools meant the beginning of the end for the native system of education.[5]

Dyzart National School, Dysart, County Louth. An early schoolhouse built in 1835.

Schoolhouses were established, often with the backing of a wealthy local patron such as an amenable landlord or a wealthy local church, or sometimes by the establishment of a school board that raised money in the locality. The national school system was intended to be financed jointly from central funds and local sources. From the beginning, local sources never matched the sums envisaged,[6] particularly (but not exclusively) in the poorer rural parts of the country (later known as the Congested Districts (see page 16)). The result was a proliferation of simple schoolhouses built in poorer areas during the latter part of the nineteenth century. These were built to standard design with little embellishment, and, more often than not, it would be these schoolhouses constructed in traditionally poorer areas that were abandoned.

Prior to 1831 the First Report of the Commissioners of Irish Education Inquiry, published in 1825, showed how the British attempt to use education as a tool of social control – endowing Protestant societies so that they provided elementary education for Catholic lower classes – had had little success. The report concluded that the origin of most of the sectarian violence that plagued Ireland was caused by educating Catholic and Protestant children separately and recommended that in future public money should be given only to schools where Catholic and Protestant pupils were taught together.[7] Therefore, the national school system was set up not only with the aim of achieving the literacy of the lower classes but also 'to cultivate good feeling between the parties that may have been at variance' while introducing religious education without causing any animosities.[8]

And so, in 1831, Earl Stanley, Chief Secretary for Ireland, outlined the new state-supported system of primary education (this letter remains the legal basis of the system today). The two legal pillars of the National School system were that children of all religious denominations were to be taught together in the same school, but with separate religious instruction.

There was to be no proselytising in this new non-religious system. Though it was initially well supported by the religious denominations, it quickly lost their support and, as mentioned above, the non-denominational aspect of primary education would slowly become a reality in law only, and not in practice. Nonetheless, the population showed great enthusiasm and flocked to attend these new national schools. At this time, the National Board put great emphasis on teacher training. Ireland was not short of teachers or schools: anyone could open a school and expect a modest income. There was exponential growth in the number of national schools through the 1830s and 1840s in Ireland. In a mere sixteen years, the number of schools in operation rose from just shy of 800 in 1833 to just over 4,300 in 1849.

By 1900 there were almost 8,700 national schools open and educating children on the island of Ireland, with close to 746,000 pupils enrolled.[9] Through the second half of the nineteenth century, first the Catholic Church and later the Protestant Churches conceded to the state, and accepted the 'all religious denominations together' legal position. However, where possible, parents sent their children to a national school under the local management of their particular Church. The result was that by the end of the nineteenth century, the system had become increasingly denominational, with individuals choosing to attend schools primarily catering to children of their own religion.[10] While the legal position, that all national schools are multi-denominational, remains to this day, in actuality, the system unfortunately functions much like a state-sponsored, church-controlled arrangement.[11]

Why are there so many abandoned schoolhouses scattered across the rural Irish landscape?

With almost 8,700 national schools in operation at the turn of the twentieth century, there was clearly a thriving education system in operation at this time. So how is that 100 years later, so many of these schools would be closed and

Gurtovehy National School, Gortaveha townland near Lough Greaney in County Clare. This schoolhouse was built in 1920 to replace an earlier school building. It now lies empty by the roadside on the edge of the Slieve Aughty Mountains.

abandoned, particularly in rural areas? The answer to this question begins not long after the National Schools Act of 1831. Unlike much of Europe at this time, Ireland remained relatively unaffected by the Industrial Revolution, and most of the population continued to live in a rural environment rather than migrating to towns and cities. The clear majority of the population were subsistence farmers on smallholdings of land that they did not own. Poverty was rife throughout the country and opportunities for betterment were few. A tradition of mass emigration would emerge that would persist to the present day.

Just a decade and a half after the establishment of the National Schools Act, Ireland's population began to decline dramatically, initially triggered by the Great Famine of the 1840s. Between 1840 and 1960, the population of the 26 counties of what would become the Republic of Ireland fell from 6.5 million to 2.8 million.[12] However, this decline was primarily driven by mass emigration, and birth rates in Ireland during this time were amongst the highest in Europe. Because of this fact and despite a dramatically falling population, the need to educate significant numbers of children of school-going age remained. New school buildings continued to be required and used.

Brockagh National School,
Brockagh Lower, County Leitrim
(built 1885). A single school
desk remains in one of the
abandoned classrooms.

Of course, without the impact of the Industrial Revolution, during this time the Irish rural/urban demographic was quite different from today's, with a majority of the population living in a rural setting. Many rural parts of the island were impoverished, and to alleviate poverty and congested living conditions in the west and parts of the north-west of Ireland, the Congested Districts Board for Ireland was established in 1891. Various political machinations were in play at the time, largely in an effort to diffuse a desire for home rule (as opposed to direct rule from Britain), but the basic role of the Congested Districts Board was to alleviate poverty by paying for public works, such as building piers for small ports on the west coast to assist fishing, modernising farming methods or sponsoring local factories to give employment and stop emigration from Ireland. The efforts largely failed, and the impact of the Congested Districts Board was minimal. In time, the rural landscape would empty.

In an era before motorised transport and a transport infrastructure, the requirement was for many small national schools to which local children could walk. Hence, in 1950 there were 4,890 national schools staffed by 4,700 male and 8,700 female teachers[13] in the 26 counties, while the population remained at about 2.8 million. To place the number of national schools in operation in 1950 in context, consider that in 1998, with the Irish population passing 4 million, the number of open national schools was 3,350.

How is it that with a rising population, there could be fewer national schools in Ireland? To explain this, we can look at the change in the Irish demographic from about 1950 onward. In 1946, some 61 per cent of the population lived in rural Ireland. By 1976 the number living in the countryside was just 42 per cent and falling. Throughout the 1950s, with the population at 2.8 million, some 400,000 Irish emigrated because of the lack of opportunities for employment at home.

With the situation at its most bleak, by the beginning of the 1960s a programme for economic expansion was initiated, establishing the Industrial Development Association (IDA) which sparked an improvement in the Irish situation, the development of an industrial economy, and a shift in settlement patterns from a rural-based economy to one centred around industry and urban settlement. This saw the beginning of a true emptying of the rural Irish population into the larger towns and cities. Small farms began to be consolidated, and actions such as the 'evacuation' of many offshore islands compounded the issue even further. All the while Ireland's birth rate began to drop, becoming more in line with of the rest of Europe. When we joined the EEC in 1973, Ireland's demographic was now beginning to resemble its European neighbours. Further to this, motorised transport became more widely available and so the catchment of schools became wider, with many in rural areas being consolidated into larger multi-classroom school buildings while the smaller schoolhouses were closed and left to rot.

There are some areas where these factors were more pronounced. Areas of poor-quality land (formerly the Congested Districts[14]), which could not support a large population, were heavily depopulated in favour of urban living. Areas such as west Cork, Kerry, Connemara, Mayo, Leitrim, Roscommon, Donegal and the north midlands saw the greatest decline in the numbers of young people remaining at home. And with this being the case, the local birth rates dropped further. Through the 1960s, 1970s and 1980s, many small rural schools were shut down and abandoned. In short, changing demographics, emigration, depopulation of the rural countryside, and the changing requirements of rural settlement meant that between 1966 and 1973, the number of one- and two-teacher schools was reduced by about 1,100.

This is the story of the one-room schoolhouse in Ireland. It is a story of a changing landscape and rural decline, changing needs and requirements. The old schoolhouses that dot the landscape symbolise the ageing populations and the movement of people to urban areas. What the future might bring is difficult to say.

Architecture and meaning

Henry Glassie is a professor of folklore at Indiana University in the United States. He has published extensively on the topic of material culture, and in the 2000 he published a book that was simply titled *Vernacular Architecture*. Glassie's publication drew on his three decades of observations of vernacular architecture from around the world and showed that common buildings, and the meanings and associations attached to them, contributed to a more democratic telling of history. Glassie viewed buildings like poems and rituals, in that they realise culture and reflect in a material way the thoughts, beliefs and experiences of the people that design, build and use them. Of course, this is true about all architecture, not just the vernacular traditions. But what do we mean when we talk about vernacular architecture, and are schoolhouses vernacular structures or imposing institutional buildings?

Original architectural drawings, dated 1869, of North Yard National School, County Roscommon (National Archives).

Vernacular architecture exists everywhere there are human populations around the world. It cannot be defined as a particular architectural style, such as baroque or neoclassical, but rather a building paradigm where the arrangement of the structure is the simplest form of addressing human needs. It is a pure reaction to an individual person's or society's building needs, and has allowed everyday people, even before the architect, to construct shelter according to their circumstance. Some are the exotic products of indigenous people in places unknown to us. But others are familiar, maybe too familiar, and so are overlooked and unappreciated. This is the case with many of the schoolhouses featured here.

Vernacular buildings are composed of local materials. The meanings that lie in the selection of materials are social and economic as well as environmental, and the buildings very much reflect the local area and its people. They can tell us a lot about the people that constructed them. As Glassie states, 'culture gathers into an inner resource of association and gathers order aesthetically', by which he means that the landscape and how people view and experience the world is

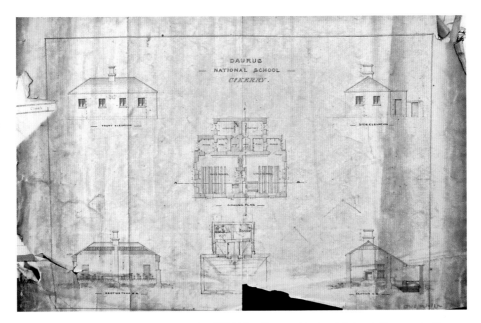

The architect's drawings supplied by the OPW for Daurus National School, Dawros in County Kerry in 1877 (National Archives).

reflected in what they build and create. With the act of physical alteration that calls time into space implying a past and a future, and with the walls that divide space, at once including and excluding, architecture has happened.[15] Architecture gives physical form to names and claims, to memories and hopes. As a conceptual activity, architecture is a matter of forming ideas into plans, plans into things that other people can see. Architecture shapes relations between people. It is a kind of a communication.[16]

But what do old school buildings say to us, and how do they tell their stories and fill the landscape with narrative? And what do the ruinous schoolhouses in rural Ireland have to say about the past? Are they examples of overbearing institutional buildings, or vernacular structures intrinsic and particular to a local community? We don't hear of these old schoolhouses being referred to as vernacular buildings but perhaps that has something to do with how we look at them and our own perspective. If we look closely we can see that they are both institutional and vernacular. They are each similar in form to each other, and usually built to a set plan supplied by a central source, the OPW. But they are constructed from local materials that are particular to each location and, on a larger scale, their designs,

An Scoil Náisunta Eiscir (Esker More National School), built in County Offaly in 1963 and now empty. This is an example of the typical, modest educational buildings constructed throughout Ireland in the 1950s and 1960s.

features and details are functional and served the basic functions required in order to provide a suitable venue for education in the rural Irish countryside.

The term 'vernacular' marks the transition from the unknown to the known: we call buildings vernacular because they embody values alien to those cherished in the architectural academy. But the physical remains of the standard 'to-plan' school buildings that lie rotting in rural Ireland are often not cherished; they are neglected. Buildings are neglected for different reasons, and pondering why some buildings get studied and others do not, we are likely to conclude that some buildings are important and others are not. Then pondering the emptiness of that answer, we find that important buildings can be interpreted as displays of the values we appreciate – grandeur, perhaps, or originality – while unimportant buildings display values that we have not yet learned to appreciate.[17] Neglect is perhaps a sign of ignorance in some way; a lack of appreciation for the important but overly familiar.

DESERTED SCHOOLHOUSES OF IRELAND

The doorway at Carrigagulla National School (Scoil Carraig an Ghiolla) in north County Cork. Built in 1934, it now lies empty on the side of 'The Butter Road' as the Cork–Tralee turnpike road was better known. The road was completed in 1748 and for two centuries or more was the main route by which farmers from Kerry and west Cork took their butter to the Cork Butter Exchange in the city.[18] Today this is a seldom-travelled back road in a depopulated part of the county, and the past importance of this route is forgotten.

Old buildings are reminders of culture and complexity. By seeing historic buildings, whether or not related to something famous or recognisably dramatic, we are able to witness the aesthetic and cultural history of an area, and thus gain a sense of permanency and heritage. This heritage comprises the physical remains of the past and also the associated stories and narratives. It can be said that no place really becomes a community until it is wrapped in such human memory: family stories, traditions and commemorations.

History and material culture are preserved in and nurture personal identity, and enable people to discover their own place in the stories of their families, communities and nation. They learn the stories of the many individuals and groups that have come before them and shaped the world in which they live. Buildings are an integral part of our material culture. Often it is only those buildings that are of historical importance or of architectural interest that are preserved and treasured, but all buildings have a story to tell.

What makes a building important?

Early publications from the nineteenth- and early twentieth-century in Britain and the US[19] provide first-hand insights into the ideological and societal backgrounds behind school architecture of the period. The significance of these buildings would later be appreciated and written about by our contemporary academics. In Britain Weiner (1994) dedicated significant word count to architecture and social reform in late Victorian London from the perspective of school design, however it was part of a thorough examination of the subject as a whole. Similarly, Avery (2003) presented a comprehensive overview of Victorian and Edwardian architecture in Britain, which included dedicated passages relating to schoolhouses designed and constructed during this period. Both of these publications looked at the physical and architectural environments in their historical contexts, offering a late-twentieth-century review of the impact of Victorian and Edwardian reform on architecture. However, neither publication was concerned with the modern-day significance or importance of these buildings to the people who engage with them now on a daily basis.

What is important to consider is that these and other studies have been primarily concerned with 'architectural interest' from an almost exclusively historical architectural perspective. They fail to draw upon or recognise the identical social significance of many similar buildings that have served the same institutional function, but were perhaps of a lesser intrinsic architectural value for a variety of reasons (date, originality of design, etc.). Hence, these buildings have been overlooked. In defining a building to be of architectural interest, Historic England (a non-departmental public body of the British Government tasked with protecting the historical environment of England) considers that to be of special architectural interest a building must be of importance in its architectural design, decoration or craftsmanship; special interest may also apply to nationally important examples of particular building types and techniques (e.g. buildings displaying technological innovation or virtuosity) and significant plan forms.

In an Irish context, the significance of early one- and two-room rural schoolhouses as vessels of cultural heritage and memory, and the narratives contained within them, has so far not been widely considered or discussed. In Ireland, the consequence of the definition supplied by the Planning (Listed

Milleen National School, Rockchapel, County Cork. Constructed in 1914, this is a fine example of a 'to-plan' schoolhouse constructed during the early years of the twentieth century. It now serves as a winter shelter for livestock.

Buildings and Conservation Areas) Act 1990 of 'architectural interest' and similar definitions, (or lack thereof)[20] is that buildings (in this case nineteenth- and early-to-mid-twentieth-century schoolhouses) that are not considered to be of intrinsic architectural importance or value are often unrecorded, even though the social role of the building through the past may be the same, and of great significance to local communities.

The above considerations indicate that there are many facets to a building's value beyond its architectural merit. This is not a new concept by any stretch of the imagination; worldwide, towns, cities and villages frequently acknowledge and highlight historical locations associated with a past event or historic personality. However, there are occasions when the social or cultural significance of a building can be overlooked, as in the case of the rural one- and two-room schoolhouses in Ireland. Viewed individually, these buildings are often considered to be of little cultural and no architectural importance. Often they have been constructed 'to-plan' according to various designs supplied by the OPW from 1831 onward, and identical buildings with chronological variations can be found all across Ireland. This fact further compounds their fate.

The perceived lack of cultural and architectural merit for individual buildings is perhaps best represented by the social circumstances and ideology that created them. Although the advent of 'education for the masses' is a characteristic of the reforming approach to education associated with the Victorian period and onward in Ireland, the associated ornate architecture of the period is not a feature of most schoolhouses constructed during this time, particularly from the latter half of the nineteenth century onward. There are exceptions to this: where schoolhouses were established with the backing of a wealthy local patron, such as an amenable landlord or a wealthy local church, original plans were often drawn up as the schoolhouse was a conspicuous demonstration of local prestige. However, by and large, the extravagance of a school's architecture was determined by the money and resources available to construct it. The intended mode of financing the national school system was that it be financed jointly from central funds and local sources. From the beginning, local sources never matched the sums envisaged,[21] particularly (but not exclusively) in the poorer rural parts of the country known as the Congested Districts (see page 16). The result was a proliferation of simple schoolhouses built to standard design with little embellishment – effectively 'factory schools'.

Hollygrove National School, County Galway (dated 1899). This plain two-room schoolhouse is a fine example of one of the most simplistic 'factory school' designs supplied by the OPW at the turn of the twentieth century. Despite their pivotal role in education in rural Ireland at the time, many of these buildings are not recorded in the National Inventory of Architectural Heritage.

This is not a strictly Irish phenomenon. It has been observed that for nearly two centuries schools have been built largely as a reflection of the factory model for learning: a homogeneous group of children in a confined space (called a classroom), process them for a year (fill them with knowledge), make sure they have learned the set and predictable curriculum (test them according to established standards), move them to the next processing container (another classroom), and continue the cycle until they have reached the age at which they are deemed ready to leave (and enter the workplace).[22] This factory model is reflected in the standardised design and architecture of these schoolhouses, and with a lack of rarity or originality in design, the building's architectural significance is today considered to be nil.

To understand and appreciate the social significance and architectural value of the now-abandoned homogeneous schoolhouses, it better to think of them not just as individual buildings, but what they represent collectively. Their homogeneous designs can be seen to represent the 'factory school' model and the ideological state apparatuses of the time; the standardisation and simplification of design reflects the standardisation of education and the curriculum, a curriculum focused on practical education and the 'three Rs'. Their internal layout (separate classrooms, entrances and schoolyards for separating boys from girls) demonstrates the legacy of their religious denominational origin and religious control of education since the nineteenth century. The location of these now-abandoned schoolhouses in the poorest and most depopulated parts of Ireland represents the changing demographics of rural Ireland over the past century. Although at first glance these are simplistic and functional buildings that are often considered unimportant, the simplicity itself contributes to the fact that these buildings are vessels of cultural heritage and memory, with narratives contained within them.

In her 2011 paper 'The Legacy of One-room Schoolhouses: A Comparative Study of the American Midwest and Norway', Leidulf Mydland draws comparisons between the social significance of historical environments of learning in the American Midwest and Norway. Her theoretical approach to the issue implied that significance, heritage value assessment and chosen narratives are a social construction dependent on the purpose which the story or the heritage object is intended to have.

It is important here once again to emphasise that many of these buildings do not enjoy legal protections on architectural merit. Their true cultural value lies in their collective significance as a shared and common environment within the diverse rural Irish landscape, which has to date been overlooked.

Drawing inspiration from Mydland's work, this book seeks to not only record and present the decaying physical remains of the disused schoolhouses in rural Ireland, but simultaneously to document the more intangible and personal significances relating to these buildings, namely the cognitive landscape that contributes to the cultural value of these buildings.

The practice of documenting buildings in ruin in various art forms is by no means new: Giovanni Battista Piranesi's etchings, and the travel sketches of Le Corbusier are all testimony to the fact that architects have long been inspired by the process of ruin that every building must eventually face in some form.[23] But only occasionally are images of the ruined buildings matched with the memories of the building's living past.

The now-empty interior of Shanvaghera National School, County Mayo, which was constructed in 1935.

340

Tramps

There are not many tramps in this district. Long ago there were a lot of tramps going about here. There is one who goes about this district regular. Her name is Ann Loftus. She is an old woman. She goes into every house along the road for a charity. She carries a can with her and into that can she puts the eggs that the people give her.

Another tramp who goes about here is Tommy Tuohy. He goes about from house to house for alms and the people give him eggs and then he prays for them.

An extract from the records of the Folklore Commissions Schools Collection at Shanvaghera in 1937 gathered by Christina O'Brien, a local schoolgirl there.

The result of this approach is, I hope, a publication that not only documents the physical and architectural significance of the disused schoolhouses in rural Ireland, but places the buildings in both their historical and present social contexts as symbols of rural decline and changing rural demographics, symbols that are significant to, and remembered by, those who attended the schools. This approach highlights the importance of these buildings as reservoirs of memory for local communities that far surpasses their lack of architectural grandeur.

Place, space and memory

Architecturally, schoolhouses vary in design from the plain and numerous 'factory school' designs, to the more elaborate and ornate schoolhouses of the Victorian and Edwardian periods that were lucky enough to have a substantial patronage. But from a more basic perspective they are constructed to provide a venue for education.

From the Lawrence Photograph Collection, Robert French's glass plate image of the classroom at Baltimore, County Cork, taken some time between 1870 and 1920. (National Archives)

The terms 'space' and 'place' have commonly been used in cultural landscape theory to describe landscapes that were produced or mediated by human behaviour in order to elicit certain behaviours and understandings of the physical environment.[24] Retrospective memories, tied to landscape (and buildings), can create the past in particular places and through social practices,[25] and places and landscape circumstances may be experienced and conceptualised at a number of levels, from personal space, to community space, to regional space.[26] Landscape may refer to the inhabited or perceived environments of human communities in the past, and may incorporate both natural and artificial elements.[27] Many forms of material culture are involved in the negotiation of identity through time, including the physical landscape and space, and both are inherently linked to socially and culturally mediated remembrance and memory of place and its significance. Thus, landscapes and places may be viewed as accumulators of memory, and can be seen as a record of past human interaction with the physical environment.[28] Quite simply put, places and spaces, through their associations with past events, act like reservoirs of memory.

My journey around the rural spots of Ireland to visit these school houses has brought to the fore many personal stories and memories. In County Leitrim, the Corraleehan Historical and Cultural Society introduced me to James and Kathleen McTague. We visited their former school, Clogher National School near Ballinamore, which they both attended as children. While inside the old schoolhouse, memories of teachers, lessons and old school pals flooded back and were eagerly shared. The building stoked the embers of memory and brought to mind the changing landscape of the area over the passing decades.

The evocative personal responses and stories relating to these buildings that the photographs I published online over the past few years were undoubtedly tied to the early childhood experiences of those who attended the schools and what these buildings represented to the individual. There is no one universal conceptualisation of childhood. It is transient and evolutionary, tempered by a number of influences, such as family and personal relationships. Even the state impacts on childhood by the provision it makes for children and families through legislation and through the provisions it makes for education, care and welfare.[29] It is this contribution in part that these buildings represented. Within the buildings, the prescribed curriculums contributed to the shape of an individual's understanding of the world.

30

The elaborate brickwork fireplace inside Drumcoe National School, built in 1938. The building is now a ruin by the roadside in south-west Donegal, not far Donegal Bay.

Although the schoolhouse as a heritage object reflects different values for different people, it is still a common symbol of a shared past within both communities and wider population.[30] It is a shared space that is recognised and remembered by all within a community through multiple generations. Memory is of the utmost importance when considering the true value of these now-ruined buildings. Memory is dynamic and fluid – a pulsing, living thing. It can be continually stretched, coveted, erased and manipulated by the environment and circumstances from which it is recalled by an individual or group – taking on greater or lesser significances that are determined by the interpretation of those who recollect in the present. Consider how much of an impact these now-rotting buildings may have had on the lives of many. The schoolhouse held notable significance as an institution for education, and represented indoctrination, ingraining the national cultural narrative and the ideological state apparatuses. It was also an environment with powerful emotional connections. These emotional connections were undoubtedly linked to the lived experience of these environments and an associated sense of nostalgia for a subsequently changed landscape.

An embroidered cross on the schoolmaster's desk at Gortahose National School, County Leitrim. This small schoolhouse was built in 1890 to serve the local rural community. Several generations went to school here before the building was closed in the 1970s.

For many who emigrated from rural Ireland at an early age, their days spent in these rural and isolated schoolhouses often represented the last formal education they received before seeking a brighter future abroad. Although many of these buildings were now empty or approaching a point of collapse, the physical structures held a wealth of memory and associations. From these small rural schoolhouses many children took what they had learned and went out to find fortune and to explore the greater world.

Although the written history of education and the architecture preserved in schoolhouses offered one facet of their historical significance, it is the emotional connection with 'place' that draws out the personal narrative of the lived experience of the schoolhouse and the rural environment.

Architecture and features of the school building

Schoolhouse designs supplied by the OPW toward the end of the nineteenth century vary in form but maintain the same basic features: an entrance porch, a cloakroom, the classroom, tall sash windows, an open fireplace and high ceilings, wainscoting on the lower parts of the internal walls, a raised wooden floor, ventilation features, etc. The architectural drawings were supplied and distributed by the OPW to all locations around the country, and for this reason you can often find identical school buildings at opposite ends of the country. There were a variety of designs supplied through the decades, and it is often possible to date the construction of a schoolhouse to within a few years based on the form of the building.

Many of the schoolhouses that were built 'to plan' were extended and modified and some remain in use today. Often a modern school building will have an original nineteenth-century construction at its core. It is interesting that many of the principal features of the early schools have been retained, such as high ceilings and windows. These features reflect the ecclesiastical and monastic origins of schoolhouse design and persist to this day. They also reflect the continuing control that Churches had on the school system.

Although there were architecturally elaborate school buildings (most often patronised by a local landowner), they more frequently comprised functional structures, usually lacking architectural ornamentation, and were built to serve a small local population.

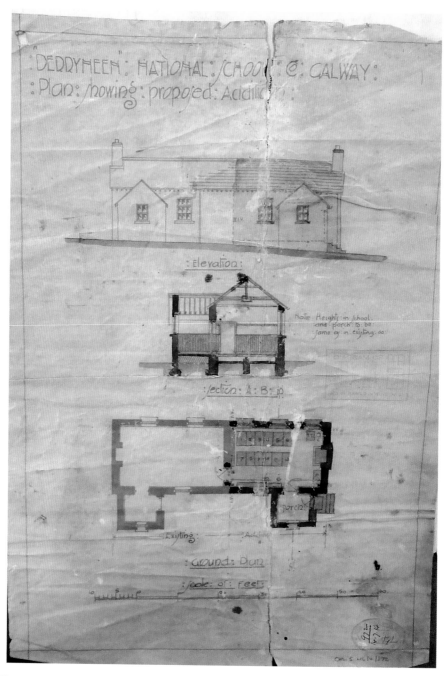

The original architect's drawings for Derryneen National School, in County Galway, drafted up in 1914 (National Archives).

DESERTED SCHOOLHOUSES OF IRELAND

The partially removed wainscoting from the walls of Lettermore National School in County Donegal, which was built in 1909.

The National Schools Act of 1831 created a demand for new school buildings in rural areas, and mechanisms to build them, and these simple structures helped to meet that demand. Many were built by local communities using local materials, but to a number of standard designs supplied by the OPW; hence there are schools of identical form scattered all across Ireland. This in itself tells the story of standardising education and providing for the educational needs of the general public; a huge and progressive leap forward at the time.

Better education was both a goal and a tool in the comprehensive modernising projects of the nineteenth century. The schoolhouse held notable significance as an institution for education and represented a shift towards better education and schooling. In reality, it cannot be overstated how significant these buildings were in bringing learning to the masses. They were at the heart of the community and remain symbolic of a more progressive ethos that stemmed from the 1831 Act.

Rural in character, for a young teacher, these buildings were often outposts of education. At times, a school might serve only a handful of families in the locality. Nonetheless, schools that children could walk to were required, and therefore many small schools with comparatively small catchment areas were

(above) The wall to the rear of Affane/Sluggara National School, County Waterford, which separated the boys' schoolyard from the girls'. This school was built in 1914; (opposite) The form, style and placement of windows vary greatly from school to school, though many early schoolhouses reflect an ecclesiastical genesis, with high pointed windows similar to those found in a church. Some were ornate and intricate, with features such as switch-line tracery. This is an example from Tubrid National School, County Tipperary and dates to 1821.

A solitary school desk within a bare
interior of Shanvaghera National School
in County Mayo. The folding screen in
the background divided the space
into two classrooms.

constructed. Prior to this, many rural areas lacked any kind of formal educational infrastructure, and these buildings represented the first steps in making a formal education available to all.

Where resources and architecture allowed, multi-room school buildings generally divided their pupils, initially by age (with infant girls and boys being taught together), before the older schoolchildren were divided by sex. Where possible, girls and boys were taught in separate classrooms, or even separate school buildings. It was not uncommon for many schools to have separate doors, or even separate schoolyard entrances for boys and girls. Often, a plaque over the doorway identified the boys' and girls' doorways. Where there were separate entrances, more often than not there were separate cloakrooms inside. The schoolyard often further enforced gender segregation, with a dividing wall running down the centre of the play area to ensure that boys and girls would not mix during lunchtimes.

Often the easiest way to identify whether a derelict building was once a schoolhouse or not is by the presence of windows that are not characteristic of

The pointed arch on a window of Porterstown Schoolhouse, in Fingal, County Dublin. The school was built in 1854 to the design of architect James Kennedy.

a domestic building. Allowing light into the building was a practical necessity before the arrival of artificial luminescence from the electric bulb. For reading and writing, high windows allowed the optimum amount of light into the room throughout the day. Even today, it is recognised that maximising the amount of natural light in a school building is beneficial to the learning environment.

When considering the ecclesiastical appearance of these windows it is worth bearing in mind that during the medieval and early modern period, in many places a monastic life was often the only avenue to literacy, and so for a long time, church and the learning environment were one. Hence, school architecture often reflects that of ecclesiastical buildings.

The presence of unnecessarily ornate architectural features often indicates a wealthy patronage of the school, sometimes by the Church, but also sometimes by a more progressive landlord, who understood the significance and importance of education. In these cases, great effort was often made to create a place of learning with stimulating and intriguing architecture. Such buildings often also reflected well on the local patronising landlord as a display of their wealth and progressive nature. The national school at Kilfinnane, County Limerick (see photograph overleaf) breaks from the 'to-plan' norm of national schools built at the turn of the twentieth century. This former school retains many of its original features and materials, such as the limestone plaque dated to 1908, copings and boundary walls, and of course, the ornate windows at the gable.

In contrast, many other schools dating to this time, which were built locally 'to-plan' following designs commissioned by the OPW, lack architectural originality, with windows often flat-headed and plain. This was perhaps a 'one size fits all' effort by the OPW that was simple and cost effective. Sash windows were the most common form of glazing, set into deep window openings like the example from Reyrawer National School, County Galway (see page 43).

It is worth bearing in mind the harsh conditions experienced by schoolchildren just a handful decades ago, when even the simplest of life's necessities could be a test of endurance. The luxury of indoor plumbing was generally beyond the expectation of most attending school at this time. When nature called, it was commonly necessary to brave the elements and venture outside to a cold and draughty detached toilet block, usually located at the rear or to the side of the already cold and damp schoolhouse. During the nineteenth and into the twentieth century, even the most basic plumbing in the outside toilet was

The ornate window at the gable end of the national school at Kilfinnane, County Limerick.

not at all common, with dry toilets being far more prevalent, particularly in rural Ireland. These dry toilets varied in form and design. Generally, a single free-standing toilet block would be located at the rear of the school building and divided for male and female pupils, and accessed through separate gender-assigned doorways. Occasionally, when a schoolyard was divided by sex, each side of a centrally located toilet block had an entrance allowing access from either the male or the female side of the yard.

Dry toilets were a simple and practical design with an absence of convenience. They comprised a number of separated cubicles over a shared trough, which could be cleared out from the rear of the building, a task that frequently fell to more hard-up members of the local community or often passing vagrants. A

Light shines through the simple sash square-headed window of Reyrawer National School, County Galway. This schoolhouse, built in 1883, is located high in the Slieve Aughty Mountains in County Galway and is reported to be the highest schoolhouse in Ireland.

The dry toilets and encroaching
greenery of Shanvaghera
National School, County Mayo.

wooden plank with an adequate opening was all that separated you from the foul quagmire below.

Some older toilet blocks opened directly onto the schoolyard, with only a simple wooden door affording any privacy.

Many early free-standing toilet blocks were later plumbed and refitted to give some degree of comfort. New-build schoolhouses and schools with extensions added from the 1930s onwards generally incorporated indoor plumbing, for example Scoil Cill Críosta in County Galway (see below).

With this added degree of luxury there was finally enough comfort to allow you to ponder over your lessons, and perhaps scribble some of your musings on the wall.

The open fireplace is an almost ubiquitous feature in every schoolhouse built in Ireland during the nineteenth and into the first half of the twentieth century. During this period, it was common for each classroom to have its own open fireplace to keep the classroom warm, though stoves could also be found in some

Autumn leaves piled high around the outdoor toilet at Scoil Cill Críosta, Ballingarry, County Galway, built in 1931. This must have been a chilly spot in winter.

DESERTED SCHOOLHOUSES OF IRELAND

schools. As part of their contribution to the upkeep of the school, the parents of pupils were required to supply fuel in the winter months (in rural schools, this was typically peat turf) to heat the classroom as needed. Generally, the location of the fireplace at the head of the classroom meant that the teacher enjoyed the benefit of the warmth much more than the children. However, as a small comfort, the fireplace was sometimes used to heat the glass bottles of milk that pupils often brought to school.

Very often, supplying turf for the school fire amounted to the schoolchildren carrying a sod or two of turf to school each morning in winter. In some cases, a family with children attending the school would provide one cartload of turf each year. When this was used up, each pupil had to bring further fuel every day until the weather improved. Turf was often stored in the porches where the children's coats hung.

It is noted by many who recall the practice of bringing turf to school that failure to supply the required fuel resulted in a caning, though officially children were not supposed to be caned for this. In 1911, government funding was made available to heat classrooms; however, the practice of carrying sods of turf to school continued for several decades afterwards.

Each morning during winter, the fireplace was cleaned of the ashes from the previous day's fire by the schoolchildren and the fire was then set. The style of the open fireplaces varies greatly from school to school though they are invariably located at the head of the classroom – be this at the gable end of the building or at an opposing central load-bearing wall that included a chimney stack. Some fireplaces included mantelpieces, hearthstones and occasional decorative brickwork, though often the hearth comprised a basic masonry or brickwork construction with little embellishment.

School fireplaces were naturally smaller than their domestic equivalents, as those included cranes and space for food preparation in the home. The schoolhouse hearth wall itself was usually very deep and extended to the ceiling, with the chimney stack protruding further above the roof. As a result of this, the chimney wall is often one of the best-preserved features of abandoned schoolhouses today.

Even today with the wonders of central heating, attending school during the cold winter months is a testing experience for many schoolchildren. Think back to what it must have been like before insulation, double-glazing and warm radiators were commonplace in the classroom.

The brightly coloured fireplace inside one of the classrooms of Ballycastle National School, Carrowkibbock Upper, County Mayo. This schoolhouse was constructed in 1892.

A textbook lies on a rotting desk in an outbuilding of Affane/Sluggara National School, Sluggara townland, County Waterford.

It is striking that for so many people who attended these schools, one of the most lasting memories is supplying fuel for the school fire.

•••••

Childhood is both a biological reality and a social construct. It is defined not only by biology, but also by a particular society at a particular time in a particular way that represents the view that society has of childhood. For example, in Ireland, we had a very different conceptualisation of childhood in 2018 than in 1918. Furthermore, our conceptualisation of childhood is different from that of society in other countries and cultures across the world. Childhood and the classroom were very different even just a few decades ago.

For boys, the turn of the twentieth century saw the introduction of a dramatically different programme and a modern approach to national school

Textbooks lie strewn across the floor of Bunglash National School in County Kerry. The discarded cassette featured *Carnival of the Animals* by Saint-Saëns, which is still part of the primary school arts education curriculum in Ireland. The school was built in 1873 and remarkably, continued in use for over a century, closing only in the 1990s.

education. In addition to the 'three Rs', inspectors' reports draw attention to the additional subjects taught: physical drill, drawing, singing, geography, grammar, history, shorthand and book keeping. For the older girls, the intensive syllabuses of instruction included cookery and laundry lessons from 1910 to 1922. Inspectors checked the cookery and laundry rolls, and usually made a note of the number of lessons given. These classes were discontinued after 1922, when – under the newly-established Irish government – curricular emphasis changed in favour of the teaching of the Irish language.

Teachers and the role of women in Irish education during the nineteenth and twentieth centuries

In the nineteenth and twentieth centuries, professional opportunities for women were, realistically, greatly restricted. Nonetheless, Irish girls and women of all social classes were leaving home to take part in public life – work, schooling, buying and selling, activism and entertainment. National school teaching was considered a great career opportunity for girls from skilled working-class and small-farming backgrounds in Ireland. On-the-job training was sometimes paid, and scholarships were increasingly available. Thus, the burden on low-income parents was bearable.

Unlike other positions in the civil service at the turn of the twentieth century, national school teaching was a lifelong job; the marriage bar (which prohibited married women from being employed in the civil service) was introduced only in 1933 for those qualifying on or after that year. At this time, the National Board put great emphasis on teacher training. This work was considered suitable for women, whether single or widowed. If they knew how to read and write, they were considered equipped to teach.

The teachers were at first treated and paid like domestic servants or unskilled labourers. Their pay was from the Board minimum, ranging from £5 a year to £16. These low figures can be explained by the informal understanding that, once appointed to a teaching post, a teacher could expect further contributions gifted from local sources. In 1858 the National Board claimed that it was paying 80 per cent of teachers' salaries, and an inspectors told teachers that if they wanted more they should apply to their own managers (i.e. the clergy). This ignored the fact that the manager could dismiss a teacher at a quarter of an hour's notice. It was recognised on all sides that teachers would have to supplement the basic allowance.[31]

The standard of education in boys' and girls' secondary schools rose in the second half of the nineteenth century, especially after the passing of the Intermediate Education Act (1878) and the admission of women to universities following the opening of the Royal University of Ireland in 1879. So by 1900 candidates for teacher training would have passed the Intermediate Certificate at about the same standard as a university matriculation. By 1900 half the newly appointed teachers had been to a training college; the other half had been monitors or pupil teachers/teacher's assistants. The latter could normally be only assistant teachers, though in a two-teacher school that was an important office, often involving teaching all the girls.[32]

However, as with most systems and institutions in Ireland during the nineteenth and twentieth centuries, the Catholic Church was dominant and controlling. The bishops refused to accept a training college not controlled by themselves with the result that in 1900, 70 years after the national school system was established, only 48 per cent of the national teachers had received any formal training. As early as 1856, the Sisters of Mercy in Baggot Street, Dublin, made efforts to give short courses to women teachers, but the six-month course was dismissed by the Powis Commission on Education as totally inadequate. In 1870 it recommended the allocation of public money towards private (denominational) training colleges. In 1883 St Patrick's Training College for men and Our Lady of Mercy Training College for women were opened and recognised, but had to support themselves. Government assistance was allowed.[33]

By the 1950s, female teachers outnumbered male teachers two to one. All this time, and almost to the present day, pay for teaching was not equal between women and men. Through the nineteenth and twentieth century all primary schools were Church-run.

The overwhelming majority were managed by the Catholic parish priest, with the rest by the local Church of Ireland parish. Successive education ministers reiterated their support for, indeed insistence on, Church control of education. This 'Catholic ethos' had a dreadful impact on the education of girls. Only a small number of girls were allowed to aim for higher education. Most were taught to read and write, sew, cook and pray. Women were educated to be wives and mothers. This education began from the day they started school. As late as 1985 the curriculum at primary level stated that: 'Separate arrangements in movement training may be made for boys and girls. Boys can now acquire skills and techniques and girls often become more aware of style and grace … while a large number of songs are suited to boys, for example, martial, gay, humorous, rhythmic airs. Others are more suited to girls, for example, lullabies, spinning songs, songs tender in content and expression.'

The gender-segregated nature of many Irish schools is part of the legacy of the denominational origin and control of education since the nineteenth century. However, even today, Ireland is unusual in a European context in that a large number of schools are still single-sex institutions at both primary and second level (42 per cent of second-level students attend single-sex schools, the majority of these being girls.[34]

In terms of extracurricular activities in the past, music and arts were traditionally encouraged to a greater degree in single-sex girls' schools, while sports (particularly field and contact sports) were of greater importance in boys' schools.[35]

There was a shift in emphasis in the 1960s from education as a social expenditure to an investment in the individual and society as a whole, and an economic boom facilitated increased investment and interest in education. Increased contact with organisations such as the UN, UNESCO and the OECD removed the insularity that had characterised Irish educational policy since the 1920s and facilitated a growing realisation of the need to invest in education for Ireland to compete on an increasingly international stage. However, although gender-segregation is much less common today, the architecture of many nineteenth- and twentieth-century school buildings still in use reflect the former division. Certainly, the majority of the schools that I have photographed echo the past paradigm of firm gender segregation. Now seen as archaic and outdated, was there ever any merit to this canon, or was it simply another reflection of denominational control of the Irish education system through the decades and centuries?

The Schools' Collection

Before we leave this section of the book, I would like to add this little note about the Schools' Collection of the Irish Folklore Commission. Throughout the following pages, I frequently refer to this primary source.

In 1937 the Irish Folklore Commission, in collaboration with the Department of Education and the Irish National Teachers' Organisation, initiated a revolutionary scheme in which schoolchildren were encouraged to collect and document folklore and local history from the eldest or most knowledgeable members of their household. Over a period of eighteen months some 100,000 children in 5,000 primary schools in the twenty-six counties of the Irish Free State collected folklore material in their home districts. These first-hand stories, poems, recipes, phrases and local folklore were all written down by the schoolchildren who attended these schools in the 1930s, and represent a wealth of local first-hand knowledge that dates as far back as the mid nineteenth century. Many of the schoolhouses featured here have complementary documents of stories.

Carrigan National School

Carrigan, County Cavan (dated 1897)

Carrigan townland is situated in the parish of Ballintemple in County Cavan. Here, just off a small country roadside, are the remnants of a late nineteenth-century detached, U-plan, single-storey school, built in 1897.

The building includes the typical double entrances, one at each end for boys and girls, with the schoolyard to the rear also being segregated. A stone plaque to centre of the front elevation is inscribed 'CARRIGANS NATIONAL SCHOOL / 1897 / ENLARGED BY REV T. MAGUIRE CC / 1929'.

The slightly ajar door allows in some light.

A bare classroom painted blue with just a single bench remaining.

It would appear that the original construction comprised a two-room school with two further classrooms added to the rear in 1929.

The two front classrooms each had tall windows in pairs of three, and, though faded now, the walls were once brightly coloured.

This is a late-nineteenth century school retaining many historic features, including original grouped windows in raised position, carved rafters, and a characteristic stone plaque. The dual entrances and divided yard reflect the gender-segregated nature of primary schooling in the nineteenth and early twentieth centuries.

Attending school here in Carrigan from 1970–78, one local woman remembers how: 'we used to bring a few turf to school at times to keep the stove going. We used to bring glass bottles of tea for lunch and line them up around the big

DESERTED SCHOOLHOUSES OF IRELAND

An internal door with all glazing missing.

'Could the last one to leave please shut the door?'

pot-bellied stove to keep them hot. There was no running water and we loved to be picked to go to the well for water. As for the toilets. Oh my God, I shiver to think about them.'

The remaining furniture inside the classroom.

DESERTED SCHOOLHOUSES OF IRELAND

Kilnaboy National School

Kilnaboy, County Clare (dated 1884)

Located near the village of Carron and the large turlough, or seasonal lake, there, Kilnaboy National School sits in a landscape rich in historical and archaeological sites, with more than 90 megalithic burial monuments in the area. However, the Burren also contains monuments from the more recent past: the vernacular architecture of the past two centuries.

Travelling from Corofin toward Leamenah, pass the little village of Kilnaboy (any fan of the *Father Ted* TV series will know this as the location of Craggy Island Parochial House). The village is most notable for its imposing eleventh-century church, visible from the roadside, and so its quaint eighteenth/nineteenth-

The exterior of the schoolhouse in late summer.

century streetscape is very often overlooked. In recent years, the former post office here has been turned into an exhibition space, aptly named 'X-PO'. And close by is a former schoolhouse, built in 1884, but now derelict and empty.

In form, it is one of the standard OPW designs of the late nineteenth century, and identical to the schoolhouses at Whiddy Island in County Cork and Gortnabinny in County Kerry: a detached, L-plan, four-bay, single-storey schoolhouse, with square-headed window openings including six-over-six timber sliding sash and casement windows. Inside, the building is bare and the remaining school furniture is stacked to one side. On the floor just inside the main doorway lies a pianola scroll.

P.J. Curtis, the present owner of Kilnaboy National School, is well known to many involved in the Irish music scene over the past forty or more years. He has produced some of the most renowned folk and traditional music albums of the past decades. He is a celebrated author and playwright, researcher and lecturer. He grew up next door to the schoolhouse and attended classes here into the 1950s. His family had sold the land that the school was built on to the school

The interior of the school with the original fireplace inside the entrance.

A pianola scroll.

board in the 1880s, and when a new school was built in 1952, they bought the land and building back. For him, this building is alive with memories: some fond and some not so fond. There are stories of camaraderie and childhood friendships, and of over-strict disciplinarians and heavy-handed discipline. P.J. is naturally reflective, and in this room his stories are all the more vivid.

He has recently begun maintenance work on the building to prevent its condition from deteriorating further. Amazingly, the building has not been recorded in the National Inventory of Architectural Heritage (NIAH), despite the fact that the identical schools at both Whiddy Island (see page 81) and Gortnabinny (see page 141) in Cork and Kerry respectively, have been. This discrepancy is a noticeable, recurring problem in the NIAH for Ireland; from county to county, there are inconsistencies in the recording and inclusion of architectural heritage in the NIAH. Thus the condition and future of this building lies in P.J.'s hands. It is an evocative place for him and for many local people, and he would not like to see it fall to disintegrate entirely.

This is an appealing national school building of compact plan and balanced proportions, built to a design prepared by the OPW on behalf of the Department of Education. The school is of particular significance as it is one of the earliest surviving purpose-built educational facilities in the Burren locality.

Milleen National School

Milleenduff, County Cork (dated 1914)

The village of Roundwood in County Wicklow claims that at 238 metres, theirs is the highest village in Ireland. However, in recent years, the denizens of Meelin in County Cork have erected a signpost at the edge of the village, stating, 'Welcome to Meelin – Ireland's Highest Village'. The folk of this tiny hamlet in north-west Cork claim that their little settlement, located just south of the Mullaghareirk Mountains, is 15 metres higher than its Wicklow rival. If you investigate the issue online, you might find various reasons why one village believes the other's claim to the title of the most elevated settlement is illegitimate. In all honesty,

The internal doorway inside the hall. Plaster crumbles from the walls

Brickwork exposed on the external corner.

the argument could probably be settled in minutes by pulling out an Ordnance Survey map – but what's the fun in that?

Meelin is one of a handful of small villages located north of Newmarket near the spot where Counties Cork, Kerry and Limerick meet. The area is sparsely populated, though the coniferous woodlands are filled with ruined cottages and farmsteads, which act as a reminder that there was a time when the lands here were farmed rather than planted with commercial forests.

It is here amongst the plantations of lodgepole pine and Sitka spruce just north of the village of Rockchapel that you will find the now disused old Milleen National School in the townland of Milleenduff. The building is hidden from view by mature evergreens, with the Caher River flowing just to the south. On a bright day, sunlight flashes through moving branches onto the south-facing gabled entrance with its centrally placed name and date plaque.

Old Milleen National School was built in 1914 and is identical in form to Scoil Bhride Culaidh, Cooly townland, County Donegal (see page 104): a simple, detached, three-bay, single-storey national school on a T-plan with a gabled projection to the front elevation and two entrances (one for boys and one for girls?) to the sides of the projection. Like other schoolhouses of this date, the schoolyard is also segregated for boys and girls. Unlike Scoil Bhride Culaidh, old Meelin National School is in a poor state of repair both inside and out. Inside, the wainscoting has peeled from the walls, while the fixtures and fittings are strewn across the interior.

Milleen is a one-room building, separated into two classrooms by a folding screen. The screen remains in place and is probably the best-preserved feature of the school building. The exploits of local teens are delicately graffitied on the wooden panelling of the screen.

There are open fireplaces at each gable, with the chimney projecting externally rather than there being a chimney breast inside the classroom. To each side of the fireplaces are tall, six-over-nine sliding sash windows. Those in the western gable retain some of their glazing, while at the eastern gable, the window panes have been replaced with Perspex to keep the encroaching greenery outside.

The building is largely a rubble-and-mortar construction. However, at the external corners, the render has fallen away to reveal the brickwork quoins.

Built in 1914, old Milleen National School is featured in the Folklore Commission's Schools Collection from 1937/8. Below is a locally recorded

The folding screen which divided the internal area into two classrooms, one for boys and one for girls.

Dappled sunlight on the date plaque.

extract from this collection, which details hedge schools in the area before the establishment of a national school.

The old schoolhouse at Milleen is in a setting similar to those at Réidh Reamhar (Reyrawer) (see page 127) and Sonnagh Old (see page 121): a forested landscape that was once farmed but is now sparely populated and dominated by commercial forestry. These forests hide a depopulated vernacular farming landscape that is barely 50 years out of use. It was the rural population of this landscape that required and facilitated old Milleen National School until it went out of use in the 1960s.

Hedge schools.

Before the national schools were established in Ireland over a thousand years ago, there were some schools all over Ireland. These schools were called hedge-schools. In some cases these schools were held only during the Winter months. The schools used to be held in an old cow house, or in a farmer's house, or out in the open air. Some of the schools used to be held out in the barns, or else in a farmers back yard. There used be only a little furniture in those schools. There used be a few seats, and a few chairs, and in some of the schools, there used be only a couple of big stones, and the scholars used to do their sums, and their writing, and all their subjects on their knees

Extracts from the Folklore Commission's Schools Collection for Milleen National School. (Folklore Commission's Schools Collection (roll number 5478)

There were no maps, or no blackboard in those hedge-schools in the older-times. There were different kinds of books in those hedge-schools. The scholars used to have their pencils, and pens. The pens that they used to have were made out of goose-quills. Each scholar used to carry his own bottle of ink, tied in the button hole of his waist-coat. Each scholar used to carry a slate and a pen made from a goose quill.

When the master would go into the school he used to strike the wall with a stick, and he would say to the scholars, "Rehearse and make noise". The more noise they would make, the people would hear them when they would be passing by. Then the people would think that they were great scholars. The school master used to stay at the farmers houses for a few nights. The hedge-school masters used to get but very little pay. They used to be kept, and fed at the farmer's house where they would be sleeping. He might stay only a few nights at each house. The best hedge-school masters came from the county Kerry. The old hedge-teacher who came to this locality was named "Cos Suinn." When the national schools were established in Milleen, a number of vagrant teachers, called at different times to the schools, and the teacher would give them a shilling for the road.

Some of the teachers were well informed men, but others of them knew but very little. "Cos Suinn" held a school in an old cow house belong to Ned Collins in Milleen. These house were not at all fit for the purpose. There was no order kept, and the school was generally the scene of noise and confusion. Still the pupils were taught to read and write. Many of them would be illiterate if it not for the work of the hedge-teachers.

Carrigagulla National School

Carrigagulla, County Cork (dated 1934)

There are few counties to rival Cork for the scale of its post-medieval and industrial heritage. And near Macroom, in the townland of Carrigagulla, there is an obscure and understated industrial project from the mid-eighteenth century.

Carrigagulla is surrounded by the amphitheatre of foothills of the Boggeragh Mountains. Here, adjacent to the Millstreet–Rylane road, are the ruins of Carrigagulla National School. The road has its own story to tell about life in this rural area during the eighteenth and nineteenth centuries: the Cork–Tralee turnpike road, better known as the 'Butter Road', was completed in 1748. Its construction was undertaken by John Murphy of Castleisland, who built the 56 miles of road, including 9 large bridges, 15 small ones, a toll house and turnpike gates. It was a requirement of the construction that the road be 30ft (9.14m)

The numbered coat hooks inside the front porch.

An external view showing the partially collapsed roof.

wide, with drainage ditches and a 15ft (4.57m) wide gravelled surface. It became the main route by which farmers from Kerry and west Cork took their butter to the Cork Butter Exchange in the city.[36]

The turnpike system was introduced into Ireland in 1729. Intended to provide good inter-county roads, turnpike roads were built and maintained by trusts, which were generally run by local landowners. The Turnpike Act empowered named trustees to erect gates and toll houses on the roads and provided a loan for their construction. The toll monies, collected from all but pedestrians and local farmers who used the roads daily, were intended to maintain the road and repay the loan.[37]

The Cork–Tralee turnpike road is today but a back road, with the majority of traffic passing along the N22 between Cork and Kerry. The area is quiet, the hills are either forested or bare and boggy, and the once bustling highway is often empty of traffic. However, at Aghalode Bridge, and adjacent to the Aghalode River, there is an old schoolhouse that is perhaps a reminder of a more thriving time in this rural spot. On the west side of the Butter Road you will find the remains of Carrigagulla National School.

The fading blue internal door.

A squadron of wasps in a disused air vent.

Constructed in 1934, it is a simple, detached, two-bay, single-storey national school on a T-shaped plan, having a gabled projection to the centre of the east elevation. Though still roofed, it is in a poor state of repair. From outside, the building is certainly institutional in appearance; the rough grey rendering is not inviting, the surrounding schoolyard is overgrown, and the foreboding hum of a wasps' nest deters visitors. The dull-green, peeling paint on the window frames and 'rainwater goods' (i.e. drainpipes and gutters) only seem to emphasise the building's predicament.

Peer through the broken glazing of the timber-framed, sliding sash-windows and see that this is another one-room schoolhouse, identical in form to the example at Lettermore in County Donegal (see page 109). Although there is just one room, it was once divided into two classrooms by a glazed, wooden folding screen. The yard to the rear is also divided. Inside, on the walls of the entrance hall, the numbered coat hooks remain.

Although no longer in use, this simple rural school has retained its architectural integrity and detailing, including timber windows, fireplace and slate roof. It represents an important part of the social heritage of the area, having served the rural education system for the first half of the twentieth century.

DESERTED SCHOOLHOUSES OF IRELAND

Cloghboola National School

Drishane, County Cork (dated 1868)

Driving south from Millstreet to Macroom in west Cork, and just past Kilmeedy Bridge, you pass the rural village of Cloghboola. Nestled in low hills, today the village comprises just a few scattered houses and the modern local national school. However, east of the road lies a curious derelict nineteenth-century building with two defunct 1950s petrol pumps outside.

Dating to 1868, this neglected structure is in fact a two-room schoolhouse. With a detached cruciform plan, this school is not of conventional design like many of standard plan from a little later in the nineteenth century. It is a single-storey school, having four bays to projecting long faces and three bays to projecting short faces.

A view of the built-in cupboard and doorway within the classroom.

The fading paint peeling from the internal walls.

The 1950s petrol pump outside the schoolhouse.

The building has a slate roof, hipped to the front long face and double-hipped to rear. It retains its original cast-iron 'rainwater goods' (i.e. drainpipes and gutters) and clay ridge tiles. The walls are rendered, and there is a render plaque to the centre of the front elevation. It includes square-headed window openings with some tooled limestone sills. These window openings are blocked to the front and south elevation, though to the rear, nine-pane fixed timber windows are evident.

Within the classrooms are built-in cupboards. In recent times graffiti has been added to the fading orange paint on the internal walls. Apart from the graffiti, the walls also include the twin dado rails common to most nineteenth-century schools. To the rear of the building is a separate toilet block of coursed rubble-stone walls, also common to schools dating from this period.

Although it is unclear, it seems the flat-roofed porch addition to north-west corner served as a kiosk when the complex was in use as a petrol station. To the front of the building are two painted metal Beckmeter fuel pumps with chrome trimmings, *c.* 1950.

In addition to the architectural interest of the building, this small school was undoubtedly of great social importance to the local community.

Some choice graffiti within one of the classrooms.

Whiddy Island National School

Trawnahaha, Whiddy Island, County Cork (dated 1887)

Whiddy Island is a small, near-shore island at the head of Bantry Bay in County Cork. Not far from the modern quayside and in the townland of Trawnahaha is a small late nineteenth-century one-room schoolhouse overlooking Bantry Bay below. Painted bright blue, with a white lime-wash, in recent years the building had been used as a local museum though it has now fallen into a state of disrepair.

Like so many of Ireland's islands, Whiddy's permanent population has dwindled over the course of the twentieth century and can no longer support a local national school. From its peak of 729 in 1841, the population gradually fell to 20 in 2011.[38]

The schoolchildren of Whiddy Island in the 1930s. This photo hangs on the hall of The Bank, the only pub on the island.

The interior of the
classroom painted blue.

Until 1880 the island had a resident population of around 450, engaged in fishing and small-scale farming. Today's population of about 20 permanent residents is augmented with seasonal visitors to the many holiday homes on the island. Though tourism and visitors to the island help to support the local economy, there is no longer a sufficient population to support a local national school. Any children of school-going age attend school on the mainland, and so the nineteenth-century schoolhouse on the island lies empty and derelict.

The attractive building comprises a detached, L-plan, three-bay, single-storey schoolhouse, built in 1887, according to the plaque on the attached gabled porch to the front. It has a pitched slate roof with rendered chimney stack and cast-iron 'rainwater goods' (i.e. drainpipes and gutters). The windows are square-headed openings with six-over-six timber sliding sash and casement windows and concrete sills. The porch includes a square-headed door opening with the original timber battened door approached by a flight of concrete steps. The complex is enclosed by rubble-stone walls and piers with a wrought-iron gate.

The fireplace within the national school. The schoolhouse served as a local museum for a period after its closure.

DESERTED SCHOOLHOUSES OF IRELAND

Light peeks through the open doorway.

Some of the original furniture remains inside.

The second edition Ordnance Survey sheet from the early twentieth century shows what was probably a toilet block to the rear of the building at the end of a large, divided schoolyard. The porch/cloakroom retains its original fittings including a built-in cupboard with coat pegs.

By 1947 there were fewer than seven children enrolled and the school was eventually closed on 31 December. In the nearby Bank pub, a photograph hangs on the wall showing Whiddy Island schoolchildren and their teachers in the 1930s. The schoolhouse is undoubtedly an interesting reminder of a time when the island population was large enough to require a school.

DESERTED SCHOOLHOUSES OF IRELAND

St Michael's National School

Slievereagh, County Cork (dated nineteenth century)

The ruins of St Michael's National School, Slievereagh can be spotted when driving from Killarney to Cork on the N22, about 2.5km before the village of Ballyvourney in County Cork. The schoolhouse is just north of a realigned stretch of road, away from the modern carriageway. From the roadside, this detached, four-bay, two-room school building stands amid open, rough grazing. It is grey and weather-beaten, with boarded-up windows and a collapsing roof.

The numbered coat hooks inside the back entrance of the schoolhouse.

Nature is creeping in through every available opening, with nesting birds now being the main occupants of the collapsing structure. Most notable in the hallway are the heavily corroded, numbered cast-iron coat hooks and fine tiled floor. From the hall, two small classrooms with matching fireplaces can be accessed. Inside, the few remaining school desks have collapsed through the remnants of the suspended timber floor.

The roof slowly collapses in the damp air around Ballyvourney.

DESERTED SCHOOLHOUSES OF IRELAND

A desk falls through the rotting floor inside one of the classrooms.

Coolmountain National School

Coolmountain, County Cork (dated 1945)

A few miles north of Dunmanway in west Cork is the rural hamlet of Coolmountain. In summer, this is a particularly lush and green place, wooded and mountainous, isolated and peaceful. The land is rough but resourceful. The landscape of Coolmountain seems to have retained an authentic rural feel: the roads are poor, the houses sparse and there is a sense of timelessness about the place.

Here, just off a small local road and partially hidden by trees, is the disused Coolmountain National School; a diminutive one-room corrugated asbestos structure that is among the more unusual schoolhouses in the country.

A view of the corrugated-iron schoolhouse hidden away in Coolmountain.

The ruins of Coolmountain National School comprise a detached gable-fronted three-bay single-storey school, built *c.* 1945. It has a pitched asphalt roof with cast-iron 'rainwater goods' (i.e. gutters and drainpipes). The windows comprise square-headed openings with metal casement windows and timber sills. It also has a square-headed door opening with a timber battened door, overlight and concrete steps. There are also rendered walls to the front and sides of the plot and a wrought-iron gate. The building ceased being used as a school in 1969 but was lived in until 2005. It is near collapse and unlikely to survive much longer.

Though constructed in the 1940s, there has been a school at this site since the 1830s. Lewis' *Topographical Dictionary* of 1837 records that:

> There are four National school-houses in the parish; three were erected by the R. C. clergyman and his parishioners, one at Kilbarry, one at Inchegeelagh and one at Ballingearig; the fourth was built at Coolmountain in 1836, in aid of which the Commissioners of Education granted £30. They also gave a gratuitous supply of books, as a first stock, to each of these schools, and continue to furnish them with books and school necessaries at half price; they also grant an annual sum of £40 towards the salaries of the teachers: the average attendance of children, both male and female, at these four schools, is 500. There is also a private school, in which are about 20 children, and a Sunday school.

According to Jerome Kelly, from the nearby townland of Clogher, the original school at Coolmountain was built in 1835 for the sum of £50. It burnt down in the early 1940s. Following the fire, pupils were temporarily schooled in a cottage in Clogher while the school was being reconstructed. The cottage was owned by a Mr Murphy. Jerome's older brother, Michael, started school in 1943 in that cottage.

Jerome Kelly himself started school in the 'new' school building on 23 August 1949. He remembers that a plaque over the door of the new building had a date of 1945 on it, probably the year that the rebuilt school opened. The new build comprised a one-room structure with a porch. There were two dry toilets. The building was heated by means of a small cast-iron stove – students themselves brought in the fuel.

Debris from when
Coolmountain National
School was lived in.

Gola Island National School

Gola Island, County Donegal (dated 1880–1900)

North-west Donegal is possibly about as remote as you can get on the island of Ireland, and the islands off the Donegal coast are as isolated a spot as you will find. Many do not have permanent populations, and if you ever need to get away from it all, this is the place for you.

Gola (in Irish *Gabhla* or *Oileán Ghabhla*) is a small island off the coast of Gweedore. The island measures 424 statute acres, with mildly hilly terrain. It is a haven for artists, birdwatchers, photographers and walkers, and the cliffs on the north side of the island attract many rock climbers. Near the island's lake, bird life abounds; cormorants, razorbills and guillemots, as well as gannets and kittiwakes, can be admired. Although many Irish people may not realise it, they

A view from the schoolhouse window toward the mainland.

may be familiar with Gola Island through song: it is the birthplace of renowned Irish writer Seán 'ac Fhionnlaoich, and the island has also been immortalised in the traditional children's song *Báidín Fhéilimí* ('Féilimí's Little Boat').

For centuries, a couple of hundred people eked out a living on Gola from fishing and subsistence farming. By the 1950s, however, the island could no longer compete with the economic opportunities offered by the mainland. Gradually, Gola's families stripped their houses, boarded their boats and sailed away to the mainland. The closure of the island's national school in 1966 marked the beginning of the end, according to Síle Uí Ghallchóir who was one of the last pupils at the school.

Since the 1960s onward, the trend on most of the offshore islands has been one of population decrease. In fact, during the 1950s and 1960s, many of the smaller islands were evacuated by the Irish government, as continuous bad weather meant that islanders were unable to travel to the mainland for several consecutive months. The most recent census, taken during 2016, showed fifteen permanent residents on Gola, although the return of permanent settlement to the island is a recent phenomenon; the island has been largely unpopulated since the late 1960s. In 2005 the island was connected to mains electricity for the first time, and from being totally deserted over 30 years ago, Gola now has electricity and a water supply, and the future looks far more positive. However, the population remains small and somewhat seasonal.

Located on the shore, the old schoolhouse on Gola is in a most precarious position, with coastal erosion threatening to erase the structure from the landscape. Stormy weather in recent years means the sea now comes right up to the door at high tide. It is weather-beaten, the roof has collapsed and in all likelihood it will be completely washed away in the coming years. (Such was the fate of the old schoolhouse on Scattery Island off the coast of County Clare.)

A plaque by the front of the building once bore the name of the school, and perhaps a date, but this has been weathered away. The original deeds for the school still exist, and date the earliest school on the site to 1846. However, the present building seems almost certainly to be of a later date, perhaps around the turn of the twentieth century. All that stands now are the bare walls of the T-plan building. Drawing architectural comparisons with similar schoolhouse designs, such as those at Bunbeg/Knockastolar (see page 99), on the mainland, and on Whiddy Island in County Cork (see page 81), we can infer that this

A view of the schoolhouse with
Mount Errigal in the background.

building was probably constructed sometime between 1880 and 1900. It appears on the first edition 25-inch Ordnance Survey from the turn of that century.

With a peak population of 169 in 1911, the two-room schoolhouse undoubtedly served the community adequately. Such diminutive schools were commonplace on the small islands during the early part of the twentieth century. In fact, early historic mapping shows some 40 national schools located off the coast of Ireland at this time. Many had just a handful of students, for example at Inishmurray in County Sligo and Island Eddie off Kinvara in County Galway.

However, these small offshore national schools are now a feature of past settlement patterns, with many of these islands now unpopulated, making the potential fate of Gola National School all the more poignant. Recently, the schoolhouse was purchased and there are plans to rescue it.

Floor tiles inside the porch of the school, stained by sea spray.

DESERTED SCHOOLHOUSES OF IRELAND

Knockastolar National School

Knockastolar, County Donegal (dated 1880–1900)

A relative stone's throw from Gweedore and Bloody Foreland is the village of Bunbeg. Just outside the little village in the townland of Knockastolar, and perched above the road from Bunbeg to Dungloe at a Y-junction, is a schoolhouse lying empty, painted in the green and yellow of Donegal. Its date plaque was missing, although its form suggests it is a late nineteenth-century schoolhouse with a later extension perhaps. The original section of the building is identical to the old schoolhouse on Whiddy Island off Bantry Bay in County Cork (dated 1887) (see page 81), with an entrance porch to the side.

A view from the entrance hall into one of the classrooms.

Inside, the building is in varying states of disrepair. The L-plan school has three classrooms beyond its entrance hall. The later classroom to the rear is in the best condition, although the blue wainscoting bears the marks of some teenage gatherings.

Both classrooms to the front and in the original part of the building are in a poor state, the floor having crumbled and the roof nearing collapse. Both these classrooms contain fireplaces, though nearly all other features have been destroyed and the wainscoting removed.

Bunbeg and Knockastolar are remote and, like much of this part of the country, do not receive anywhere near the amount of visitors that topographically similar spots like Connemara and west Kerry do. At Bunbeg there is a tiny fishing village hidden in a cove behind an expansive strand, overshadowed by Errigal in the background. The area is a mountainous Gaeltacht that drops to the sea and is dotted with dozens of idyllic villages just like Bunbeg.

But despite seeming disconnected from all that troubles the world, Knockastolar National School produced at least one famous and important student who made his mark on the world during the Second World War: John

The air vent in the corner of the classroom. This was an almost ubiquitous feature of schoolhouses from this period.

An original fireplace, now destroyed.

James Doherty, who worked at Bletchley Park (Britain's top secret decoding centre) as a cryptanalyst and translator. Being from the area and attending Knockastolar National School, John was a native Irish speaker. While his other languages – German, French, Italian, Spanish, Polish, Russian, Latin and Greek – were fully utilised, he never disclosed whether his knowledge of Irish helped in Hitler's defeat.

The graffitied walls inside
one of the classrooms.

Scoil Bhride Culaidh

Cooly, County Donegal (dated 1931)

The picturesque town of Moville lies on the western banks of Lough Foyle in County Donegal where the Bredagh River flows into the sea. The locality was the adopted home of the dramatist Brian Friel, and it still attracts many visitors who make the long journey north to the Inishowen Peninsula and Ireland's most northerly point on nearby Malin Head.

At the turn of the nineteenth century there were just 50 people living in the town of Moville, but the town would rapidly develop over the following decades. During the second half of the nineteenth century, Moville was a significant point of embarkation for many travellers, especially emigrants to Canada and the USA. Steamships from the Anchor and McCorkell Lines and others en

An external view of the domineering Scoil Bhride Culaidh.

A view of the classroom with a folding glass-panelled divide.

route from Glasgow to New York, Philadelphia, Quebec and New Brunswick regularly dropped anchor in the deep waters off Moville to pick up additional passengers.

The new trade brought wealth and development to the town, and a growth in population. Naturally, the growing population would need education, and there were a number of national schools constructed, not just in the town, but in the hinterland also. The schoolhouse featured here is one such building. Scoil Bhride Culaidh is located near Cooly Cross, a rural spot just 3km north-west of Moville.

The building itself dates to 1931 but an examination of the first edition 6-inch and 25-inch Ordnance Survey maps shows that this schoolhouse replaced an earlier one, named 'Tiyrone School', just a few hundred metres to the east, marked today by an area of rough ground. This earlier schoolhouse, which dates to at least the 1840s, was, unusually, located away from the roadside, enclosed in the corner of a field. Two rights of way led to the school through the surrounding farmland. Perhaps someone still knows the reason for this school's inconvenient setting: was it perhaps built on land donated by a local landowner?

The two doorways provided separate entrances for boys and girls.

Inside, Scoil Bhride Culaidh is in good condition, with many of the original fixtures and fittings still in place, including the ornate air vents in the corners of the diminutive one-room schoolhouse. These are an almost universal feature of nineteenth- and early-twentieth-century school buildings. Lindsay Baker has briefly looked at the role of ventilation in her publication *A History of School Design and its Indoor Environmental Standards, 1900 to Today*. In its simplest form, instructions for the heating and ventilating of classrooms could be boiled down to this statement from Hamlin: 'Abundant quantities of warmed fresh air should be introduced through ducts to each schoolroom, and care must be taken that the ducts are of sufficient area and directness for passing the required amount. Ducts should also be provided for removing the vitiated air.'

Although no longer in use, this simple rural school has retained its architectural integrity and detailing, including timber windows, fireplace and slate roof. While technically a one-room building, it appears to have had separate classrooms for girls and boys, separated by a folding screen. The yard to the rear is also divided. It represents an important part of the social heritage of the area, having served the rural education system from the first half of the twentieth century.

The ubiquitous air vent.

Lettermore National School

Lettermore, County Donegal (dated 1909)

From the south-westernmost point at Mizen Head in County Cork, you need only travel about 550km to reach the northerly tip of the country at Malin Head in County Donegal. But along that journey, you will witness a variety of landscapes, both physical and cultural, each different from the other in striking, or sometimes subtle, ways. From productive mixed farmlands for both tillage and stock, to the mire of endless bog, the physical landscape has been shaped and manipulated, initially by geological process and subsequently by the people who have lived in it. Particularly in rural Ireland, the physical and cultural landscapes are intertwined and form a narrative that is often not immediately clear, that requires an insight into and interpretation of what shapes the lived experience

An external view of Lettermore schoolhouse.

The main door hangs off its hinges.

of the world around you. In short, the landscape and what it contains tell the history of the inhabitants.

The slogan 'Up here it's different' has been used to promote tourism in and attract tourists to Donegal in recent years. But what makes this area different? In terms of physical geography, it is pretty similar to west Cork, Kerry and Connemara: a rugged western coastline shaped by the Caledonian Orogeny, and battered by the Atlantic Ocean, mountainous lands of blanket bog to the west, and better, more productive lands to the east.

But Donegal is different from these other places. Depending on your perspective, the circumstances of history have not done Donegal any favours other than perhaps to help preserve its striking landscape. The partition of Ireland in the early 1920s had a huge, direct impact on the county. It cut the county off, economically and administratively, from Derry, which had acted for centuries as its main port, transport hub and financial centre. But even before this, Donegal was one of the worst affected parts of Ulster during the Great Famine of the late 1840s. Large swathes of the county were devastated by this catastrophe, many areas becoming permanently depopulated. Vast numbers of people emigrated at this time. Particularly in west Donegal, there was a spiral of decline from the 1900s onward, and what was once seasonal migration from the islands and highlands was replaced by more permanent migration to cities in Great Britain such as Glasgow.

The abandoned schoolhouse at Lettermore symbolises the recent history of the region, and the story of migration. Opened in 1909 to meet the educational needs of the local community, the school had a relatively short life.

It is a simple detached two-bay, single-storey national school on a T-shaped plan, having a gabled projection to the centre of the west elevation and a single-storey toilet block to the rear.

With little in the way of prosperity to keep people in the area, the depopulation of the 1940s and 50s saw the destruction of the area's social fabric as house after house closed, and the birth rate dropped. The closure of the border roads between southern and northern Ireland from the late 1960s on hastened the dismantling of the community.

In 1967, the school was closed as part of a programme to amalgamate four local national schools, the others being Letterfad, Derryherc and Binbane. But today, not even the amalgamated school is doing well. There were only three

A lonely teapot sits on a shelf beside a kitchen sink installed in the adjoining repurposed entrance hall.

The single room is
divided in two by a folding
glass-panelled divide.

new pupils to the new national school in 2018, with eleven leaving for secondary school in Donegal town. The trend of depopulation continues.

After closing, the building was bought by a visitor from Europe in 1972. Since then it has lain empty. Inside, time is beginning to take its toll: the wooden panelling is falling away from the stone-and-mortar walls, revealing the building's simple structure.

Although now out of use, this modest but well-built early twentieth-century national school survives in relatively good condition and retains its early form and character. Its integrity is enhanced by the retention of much of its early fabric, including natural slate roofs, timber sliding sash windows and timber doors. Its simple T-shaped plan and layout is characteristic of the great many two-classroom national schools built throughout Ireland in the late nineteenth and early twentieth centuries to standardised designs prepared by the Board of Works/OPW. National schools of this type are a feature of the isolated rural landscapes of County Donegal, adding a layer of social history to the physical environment, and are indicative of significant local population in a period when transport was more difficult.

Coolagh National School

Drumatober, County Galway (dated 1930–40)

The rural landscape is not static, and has changed substantially in recent decades. Although the hills, mountains, rivers and lakes don't move much, the way that people interact with the landscape, and the character of the environment is dynamic and fluid. Rural towns and villages, which were once important market places and hubs of rural activity, fade into a collective nostalgia for times gone by, as young people gravitate to cities, and the landscape empties.

Before motorised transport and the railway, distance was largely the determining factor when choosing a route from west to east. Travelling from

A view of one of the two entranceways, which are located at either end of the building.

Galway to Dublin by carriage or on foot, it was likely that you would take a route through Loughrea, Killmor and Eyrecourt, crossing the River Shannon at Bangher in County Offaly, all the while passing near or along a much more ancient route, An Slighe Mhór, a system of eskers that stretches across Ireland, which has been used as a natural thoroughfare since prehistoric times. More recently, the N6 took you through Ballinasloe, Athlone and on to the myriad bottlenecks nearer the capital. These old routeways are no longer frequently travelled and thus an old schoolhouse, although not far from a former major road, is all the harder to find: Coolagh National School in the parish of Abbeygormacan near Killoran is on the northern side of the N65, about 3km beyond Gurtymadden Cross when travelling east.

Coolagh National School is a late 1930s/early 1940s schoolhouse (there is no date plaque to confirm the date) with two classrooms and a hipped roof of natural slate. There is a doorway on either side of the building, and some offices and toilets located in a flat-roof extension to the rear. The functional building is set within a grassy, overgrown schoolyard set back from the nearby road.

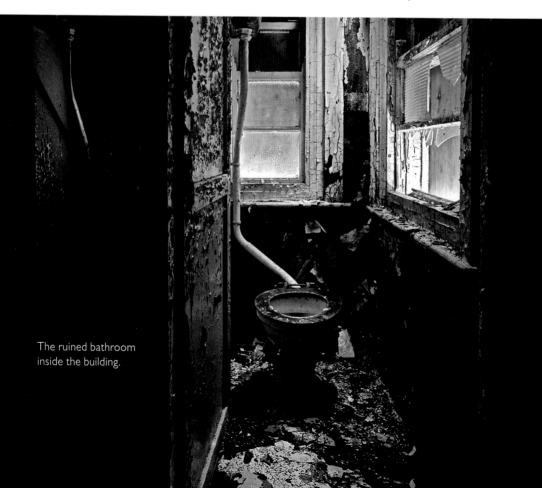

The ruined bathroom inside the building.

A view from the hallway into a classroom. Light makes its way in through the holes in the ceiling.

The skeletal remains of an organ in an alcove along the hall.

A haunting view along the corridor.

Light peeping into the old bathroom.

At the time of the first edition Ordnance Survey 6-inch and 25-inch series (1829–1842 and 1897–1913), there was no schoolhouse here. The building does not appear on cartographic sources until the Cassini 6-inch maps, which were mostly produced in 1940s, at that time called 'Coolagh School'. However, Coolagh National School is located in the townland of Drumatober, and Coolagh townland is another kilometre or so further east. If we look at Coolagh at the time of the 25-inch series, we can see that there was an earlier schoolhouse here, and it would seem obvious that the late 1930s/early 1940s building featured here replaced an earlier nineteenth-century schoolhouse.

Inside, the building is beginning to crumble and deteriorate. The ceilings are beginning to collapse and the paint is flaking from the walls. The windows are boarded up and even on a bright, warm day it is relatively chilly inside. Both classrooms have been stripped of their furnishings. At one end of the long corridor are the bathrooms (now post-apocalyptic in appearance), while at the other end of the corridor, in a small alcove, is the wooden skeleton of a long-disused organ.

Sonnagh National School

Sonnagh Old, County Galway (dated 1891)

Sonnagh National School is situated in the Slieve Aughty Hills on the border between south-east County Galway and north-east County Clare. It is one of a number of disused schoolhouses in this beautifully desolate landscape. Like Réidh Reamhar/Reyrawer National School (see page 127), Sonnagh National School stands in the low rounded hills of the Slieve Aughtys as a testament to the now-dispersed people who lived and farmed in this area in the decades past. The forested hillsides are dotted with the ruins of former farmsteads. The former pasture and rough grazing lands have been sown with coniferous plantations, and

Detail of the brickwork arch over the classroom doorway, revealed by the peeling plasterwork.

A view of the single classroom, strewn with debris and rubbish.

the ubiquitous and imposing wind turbines highlight the movement away from agrarian living here, as an alternative and profitable use is sought for this now people-less landscape. The result is an empty, desolate place. An unintended but welcome consequence of this depopulation is the creation of a retreat from the ribbon development popular across much of the Irish landscape, although the tree plantations bear a haunting watermark of former settlement, with field boundaries, boreens, houses, farms and infrastructure, such as disused schools, hidden throughout the forests. When Sonnagh National School was in use, this was a lived-in landscape that supported a scattered, largely agrarian population. With the movement away from this lifestyle, the landscape was emptied and the school was no longer needed. The plaque on the eastern gable of the building dates the construction of the school to 1891. It closed in the late 1950s.

The bright-red brickwork fireplace at the head of the class.

This rubble-and-brick construction, situated in the forestry plantation to the north of Francis Gap, is a detached, single-storey, three-bay, one-room schoolhouse, with a pitched slate roof. The fireplace is at the southern end of the building and there is a collapsed dry-toilet block located to the west and rear of the school building. Most aesthetically pleasing, though in a ruinous state, is the adjacent schoolmaster's house to the north.

The plaque on the eastern wall dates the building to 1891. However, the first edition Ordnance Survey (1829–1842) sheet shows that it was not the earliest schoolhouse in the area, with a schoolhouse marked at another location 500m north of here on the Francis Gap road.

The building is in a poor state of preservation today, with the suspended floor now collapsing. Inside, it is strewn with domestic rubbish, though a single original school desk remains.

A copy of *Woman's Own* lies on a window shelf.

Parallels can be drawn between the recent development of the landscape of the Slieve Aughtys and other parts of Ireland where the lands have become depopulated in the second half of the twentieth century. Regions such as northwest Mayo, parts of Galway, Leitrim, parts of Clare, Kerry, Cork, and so many other rural areas around Ireland are being reclaimed by forestry plantations. It is an echo of similar population dispersal and land clearance on a grand scale in the

Scottish Highlands centuries beforehand, where sheep replaced tenant farmers in the landscape to ensure an income from vast estates of rough land thought to be of low productivity. This population displacement created Scotland's expansive and breath-taking wilderness to the north. It is a bittersweet circumstance. Although the creation of wilderness is welcomed, is it being done with a holistic vision of both the cultural and physical landscape? Are these anthropogenic, rectilinear forests being superimposed on the landscape without appropriate regard for cultural heritage in an effort to make them profitable? And should a greater effort be made to blend these forests with the natural and cultural landscape? Are important but unrecognised elements of our cultural heritage being swallowed up by forestry plantations?

Light through the doorway

Réidh Reamhar (Reyrawer) National School

Reyrawer, County Galway (dated 1883)

Reyrawer National School is situated in the uplands of the Slieve Aughty Mountains in the parish of Peterswell (Kilthomas) in south-east County Galway, and is considered locally to be the most elevated schoolhouse in Ireland, at 225m OD. This is quite a claim and it is yet to be confirmed. Today, the elevated aspect from the doorway of the schoolhouse, which is surrounded by the coniferous forestry plantations, affords excellent views of the karst landscape of the Gort lowlands to the south. Despite the fact that the uplands are today abandoned, there is a maze of small roads and field boundaries through the forest lands and across the fresh hillside. The 1911 census shows fourteen families living in the townland of Reyrawer (meaning 'thick field' or 'mountain plain') at that time. Nonetheless, there is now a great sense of emptiness here. With many of the vernacular houses of those who once lived here being swallowed up by the forestry plantation, the school building feels like the last reminder of the communities that once populated this area.

This is a detached one-room schoolhouse with an attached entrance hall to the south. Inside, the suspended timber floor has begun to collapse, though the pitched roof remains in good condition, which protects the interior from the elements. To the rear of the main building is the former toilet block, while to the west lies the concrete schoolyard shelter, which was cast *in situ*.

Toberroe National School

Toberroe East, County Galway (dated *c.* 1901)

Toberroe National School is in the townland of Toberroe East in north Galway. Although constructed around 1901, Griffith's Valuation of *c.* 1855 shows that a portion of the lands belonging to John Cheevers were at that time exempt from taxation as they formed part of a school grounds and buildings. This indicates that an earlier schoolhouse was in existence in the townland at this time.

The earlier building can be identified on the north-eastern boundary of the townland on the first edition Ordnance Survey sheet for the area (1829–1842). The present building continued in use until 2010 and is in a good state of preservation with much of the old school furniture still inside.

A view of the rear of the schoolhouse through the long summer grass that now grows wild.

The relatively modern sinks inside the outdoor toilet block to the rear of the school.

The gateway leading to one of the two entrances.

The stone for Toberroe National School was quarried at Turlough, where stone was also sourced for the new building at Killyan House, belonging to the Cheevers in 1872. The present school building comprises a detached eight-bay, single-storey national school with separate entrances to the rear for boys and girls. It has a pitched slate roof with render eaves, red-brick chimney stacks and cast-iron 'rainwater goods' (i.e. drainpipes and gutters). The walls are rendered, ruled and lined, and there is an inscribed limestone plaque. The schoolhouse has square-headed windows with timber six-pane upper flaps over nine-pane fixed lights. There is a garden to the front bounded by a rubble limestone wall. The gateways have square piers with chamfered caps and metal gates. To the rear is the former toilet block divided for male and female children.

This school, built to a standard design, is reportedly the longest of its type in the county. Although it has fallen into disuse, it is still in reasonable condition and retains its original timber windows and many other details.

Bunglash (Bun Glaise) National School

Bunglash South, County Kerry (dated c. 1873)

On 12 September 1893 the Great Southern and Western Railway opened a branch line off the existing Tralee–Mallow line, connecting the village of Farranfore with Valentia Harbour on the southern shore of Dingle Bay. At that time it was the most westerly railway line in Europe and passed through some of Ireland's most spectacular scenery as it climbed through Kerry's mountainous

A view of the schoolhouse with the County Kerry landscape in the background and a grassed-over basketball court in the foreground.

Detail of the map that still hangs on the wall.

countryside. It served as the main transport system for the Iveragh Peninsula for 75 years, with the last train departing Killorglin on 30 January 1960.

So, for 67-odd years, a steam-powered locomotive chugged daily along the Farranfore–Valentia Harbour line, passing just north of the glacial lake Lough Carragh, and stopping at Glenbeigh Station. This station was at the foot of Seefin Mountain, and the surrounding landscape at the turn of the twentieth century was beautiful, wild and remote. There were few distractions intruding from the outside world, and the coming and going of the steam train punctuated the day. In the surrounding hills and mountains, schools did not have clocks, and the whistle of train in the quiet landscape as it passed over Curraheen level crossing at 10.15 a.m. let the local schoolchildren know that it was *am sos* ('break time').

There were six schools in the parish of Glenbeigh: Glenbeigh, Curraheen and Leitir, Bunglash, Bohesill and Shanacashel. One of these schools, Bunglash National School, is at the western end of Lough Carragh and still stands, though it is now disused.

A school desk remains in the classroom.

A battered typewriter lies on the ground.

It is a detached, two-room national school built in 1873. The form of the building is somewhat unique, or at least does not appear to be one of the easily recognisable 'to-plan' designs distributed by the OPW during the latter part of the twentieth century. It is a T-plan building with a hipped roof to the west, and a projecting gabled roof to the east with a date plaque located high on the gable end. Today, the modern pebble-dash has been painted a sober, off-white colour, and one can only wonder what the underlying original brick and stonework would look like.

Handsome and sturdy six-over-nine sliding sash windows allowed plenty of light and the mountainous views into the classrooms, though much of the glazing has been broken.

The building is in good condition, considering it is over 140 years old. Inside, there is still some of the old school furniture, including school desks and shelving, most remarkably, many of the old textbooks that were used. Judging from the many books scattered about the floor, it seems likely that children were still being taught here in the 1990s at least.

The walls of the classrooms include poster rails. Quite often these do not survive as the building begins to rot, but at Bunglash they are intact, and in the corner of the classroom, a map of Ireland still hangs. The maps shows nearby Lough Carragh and the old, now-disused railway line.

Cluain Chumhra National School

Cluain Chorta, County Kerry (dated c. 1911)

The Dingle Peninsula (or Corca Dhuibhne) in County Kerry stretches some 48km into the Atlantic Ocean from Ireland's south-west coast and is a popular spot for holidaymakers. The peninsula is dominated by mist-covered mountain ranges that form its spine, running from the Slieve Mish range to Mount Brandon, Ireland's second highest peak. The coastline consists of steep sea cliffs, broken by sandy beaches, with two large sand spits at Inch in the south and the Maharees to the north. Off the west coast lie the Blasket Islands, inhabited until 1953 when the remaining islanders were evacuated to the mainland by the

A view along the corridor.

THE
CLONARD
READERS

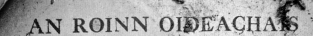
With Life, Introduction,
of Subjects for Short Essays

AN ROINN OIDEACHAIS

OIDEACHAS NÁISIÚNTA
(NATIONAL EDUCATION)

REGULATIONS

AND

EXPLANATORY
NOTES

FOR THE

...ng of Rural Science and
Nature Study

... PRIMARY SCHOOLS

...ILL'S ELEMENTARY...

GENERAL EDITOR: JAMES J. CARE...

VIRGIL
AENEID XII

BAILE ATHA CLIATH:
DUBLIN.
FOILLSITHE AG OIFIG AN tSOLATHAIR.
PUBLISHED BY THE STATIONERY OFFICE.
Le ceannach trí MESSRS. EASON AND SON, LTD., 40 agus 41 Sráid
Uí Chonaill, Baile Atha Cliath.
To be purchased through MESSRS. EASON AND SON, LTD., 40 and 4...
O'Connell Street, Dublin.

(Raol Glan.)
(Sixpence Net.)

Exam notes and
books on the floor
of the schoolhouse.

St Oliver Plunkett has remained behind after everyone else has left.

Irish government. It is an area of outstanding natural beauty, and despite a busy tourist season, it is a peaceful place that retains its rural feel.

The principal town on the peninsula is Dingle, a major fishing port. The fishing industry, which dates back to about 1830 here, brought the railways to the town, and Dingle was formerly the western terminus of the narrow-gauge Tralee and Dingle Light Railway. The railway station opened on 1 April 1891, closed for passenger traffic on 17 April 1939 and for regular goods traffic on 10 March 1947, finally closing altogether on 1 July 1953, by which time a cattle train once per month was the sole operation. The railway line wove along the south coast of the peninsula on its way from Tralee, crossing a flat, low-lying area between Lispole and An Cnoicin, known as Droichead An Imligh (Emlaghmore Bridge). It is adjacent to the former railway line and the modern N86 road in the townland of Clooncurra that you will find an early twentieth century schoolhouse no longer in use.

The building comprises a detached U-plan school with a central two-bay single-storey block flanked by three-bay, single-storey, gable-fronted traversing blocks to the sides. Built in the early twentieth century, this rural school once fulfilled an important function for the surrounding rural community. Its balanced design with gable-fronted bays gives it a strong presence within the countryside. Although disused, the building is in good repair and is enhanced by the retention of its historic slate roof, cast-iron gutters and drainpipes, timber sash windows and doors.

Inside, the building is frozen in time, and there is a treasure of old school furniture, books (though some of these appear to be from a secondary school), and bric-a-brac dating from around the time when the school closed in 1993.

A ghostly organ lurks in the corner of one of the classrooms.

Gortnabinny National School

Gortnabinny, County Kerry (dated 1880–1898)

The landscape surrounding Gortnabinny is hilly; the ferns are a lush green colour, and in the damp, heavy warmth of evening, the dense greenery and woodlands can seem tropical. About 10km south of Kenmare, this rural spot is at a gateway to the Beara Peninsula. Leaving the humid roadside, which is arched by a canopy of the most vibrant green deciduous trees, climbing up a low knoll through the wet woodlands; toward the crest of the hill the remnants of single-storey building, half-hidden behind pine palms, can be discerned.

The name plaque over the doorway.

Detail of the brickwork and the green doorway to the schoolhouse.

The whitewashed building comprises a detached, L-plan, three-bay, single-storey schoolhouse. The gable end of the projecting porch includes a name plaque which reads 'Gortnabinni National School', though there is no date. Drawing architectural comparison with the schoolhouses at Whiddy Island (see page 91), and Réidh Reamhar (see page 127), it seems likely that this school was built sometime between 1880 and 1897.

Why 1897? The school building is marked on the second edition 25-inch Ordnance Survey map (1897–1913) for the area which shows the building located on the low hill, with footpaths leading to the rear of the school where there are two outbuildings, most likely toilet blocks. It is squeezed between two small streams with only one other building nearby.

Inside, the crumbling plasterwork has revealed the appealing pattern of the roughly coursed stonework with brick quoining underneath. Although the school was built to a standard plan supplied by the OPW at the time, it was constructed of local materials, by local people.

A 1970s bathroom from when the schoolhouse was lived in.

Greenery slowly invades through the open window.

From the interior, it is obvious that this school has had at least two lives. In what was once the main classroom, there are the remains of relatively recent partition walls that divide the main room into three. The floorboards have completely rotted so all that remains is a dusty clay underfoot. A doorway leads to a smaller room, perhaps originally a classroom for infants.

The walls are covered with a peeling patterned wallpaper. To the rear of the building there is a modern flat-roofed extension. Here, there is a kitchen and bathroom with 1970s-style fittings. It must be that after its life as a schoolhouse, the building was converted to a house and lived in.

But what of the former use of this building? The patterned wallpaper and partition walls make it difficult to imagine this place as a schoolhouse. There are no school desks, no blackboard or other features of the school interior remaining. Only the name plaque on the front gable and the recognisable architectural style of the building indicate that this was once a local schoolhouse. However, a quick look through the records of the National Folklore Commission show that, in the 1930s, this building was still very much alive as a school. A fine collection of stories and folklore from the locality was gathered by the local schoolchildren at the time.

As with Reyrawer in County Galway, it is the landscape setting of this disused school that is most striking. The building is isolated now, and it is difficult to imagine a time when there were enough schoolchildren in the locality to necessitate it. Perhaps this is what makes Gortnabinny National School interesting: it is a relic of the past and a legacy of the changing rural Irish landscape of the past 50 years.

Drumreilly National School

Kilnacreevy, County Leitrim (dated 1887)

Every now and then I find myself on the road when I chance upon some old empty schoolhouse by a roadside somewhere. While travelling from Ballymote to Armagh last month, I happened across a late nineteenth-century schoolhouse in the townland of Kilnacreevy in County Leitrim.

County Leitrim is Ireland's least populous county, predominantly rural in character, with Carrick-on-Shannon the most sizeable town. However, the countryside is stunning in an understated way, defined by rolling, boggy drumlins

The ruined fireplace in the classroom.

A view into the classroom from the entrance.

interspersed with small lakes. The land is agriculturally poor, and the hollows between the drumlins tend to become waterlogged. In 1837, the antiquarian Samuel Lewis described the region as 'generally wet, sour, and moory'.

Lewis was a little unfair with his description of the region. In the area around Garadice Lough on the Leitrim/Cavan border, meandering country lanes navigate the hillocks and lakes, and lead from one small village to the next. It is on the northern shore of Garadice Lough that you will find Kilnacreevy townland, a place that has not changed much in the past century.

It was just a little over 110 years ago that a small one-room schoolhouse was built here overlooking the lakeshore. It is north of the modern R199 road. The rubble-and-brick construction comprises a detached, single-storey, three-bay, one-room schoolhouse with a pitched slate roof. The date plaque indicates that it was constructed in 1887. It is almost identical in form to the example from Sonnagh Old in County Galway (see page 121), and in a similar state of decay.

Comparing the first (1829–1842) and second (1897–1913) edition Ordnance Survey maps, you can see that the 1887 building replaced an earlier schoolhouse once located on the opposite side of the road. The 1887 building is clearly an OPW design, part of the significant school-building movement in Ireland toward the end of the nineteenth century. On the first edition Ordnance Survey sheet, there was another school beside the rectory just over a kilometre to the west, in Killaphort. Killaphort's association with the rectory here might suggest this was a Protestant school.

Although now derelict, this former school building retains much of its early character. Its simple symmetrical form is typical of the standard school buildings designed and built in great numbers by the OPW for the Board of Education during the late nineteenth century and in the first decades of independence, particularly from about 1925 to 1939. Its structure suggests that it was originally built as a one-classroom school although this impression is undermined by the boundary wall to the rear, which divides the yard into two separate enclosed spaces, indicating that the single classroom was probably once divided in two to accommodate boys and girls separately. The school retains many original features that enhance the façade, such as the slate roof, timber sash windows and the carved limestone with incised Gaelic script. This simple school building was of social importance to the local community and represents a modest addition to the built heritage of the local area.

A view from the rotting floorboards towards the head of the classroom.

Gortahose National School

Gortachoosh, County Leitrim (dated 1890)

Just a few miles south-east of the townland of Ballinamore in County Leitrim, and set amongst the rolling, boggy drumlins and frequent small lakes, is the rural village of Corrawaleen. During the first part of the nineteenth century a small schoolhouse was located in the village and is marked on the first edition Ordnance Survey map for the area. However, in 1890 a new schoolhouse was built in the nearby townland of Gortachoosh just outside Corrawaleen.

This schoolhouse still stands. Though derelict and beginning to collapse, inside it is in good condition, and the echoes of past schooling can almost be

A view of the fireplace in one of the two classrooms.

A stray school desk in the hallway.

The electric light brought luxury to rural Ireland.

The solid wood schoolmaster's desk still remains in the main classrooms.

heard amongst the scattered school furniture. In bright daylight, the schoolrooms seem vibrant still.

The building comprises a detached, four-bay, single-storey former national school, built in 1890. It has a pitched slate roof with a red-brick chimney stack, cast-iron rainwater drainpipes and gutters and timber bracketed eaves. The external walls are pebble-dashed with a date plaque to the front elevation. Most of the glazing in the timber sash windows is broken and scattered inside.

This national school building type is found throughout County Leitrim. Some of the schools are still in use in a highly altered form but this example retains its original plan and features.

Feohanagh National School

Feohanagh, County Limerick (dated 1886)

The rural landscape of many parts of Ireland is punctuated by small villages, which, for various reasons, have fallen into decline in recent decades. In west County Limerick is one such village: Feohanagh ('the place of the thistles') located 8km south-east of Newcastle West on the R522 road to Dromcollogher.

The first edition 25-inch map (1897–1913) shows that at the turn of the nineteenth century this hamlet included a smithy, post office, terraced street, church and a two-room schoolhouse. Today, no shops, post office or other services remain open here, though north of the R522 are the remains of the disused two-room national school built in 1886.

A view of the schoolhouse from the roadside.

The stove that was used to heat the schoolhouse.

Prominently sited, this former school is a pleasing roadside feature. The building comprises a detached, T-plan, six-bay, double gable-fronted national school. The school is approached from the R522 via a narrow laneway overgrown with briars. The exterior is well weathered, the schoolyard now overgrown, and in the quiet countryside of west Limerick there is an eerie silence around the ruins of this imposing symmetrical building. Although well worn, the schoolhouse retains its original pitched slate roof with rendered chimney stacks and limestone coping. The original timber sash windows also remain, though much of the glazing is now broken and scattered across the old mossy playground. To the rear of the school is the original dry-toilet block, also hidden by brambles and dense greenery.

Inside, the fixtures and furnishings are in good condition. The original open fireplaces in each classroom were replaced with oil-burning stoves. School furniture is scattered throughout, and despite the feeling that this building is from another era, it is clear that the school remained in use until relatively recently.

This schoolhouse is a reminder of life in Feohanagh in the nineteenth and twentieth centuries when the village was perhaps more vibrant than it is today. The nineteenth century in Ireland was a period of great social change, particularly in the area of education in the rural countryside. During the 1800s, education was increasingly seen as a means of preparing those children who did not inherit the land for other forms of employment or for migration. Though there was some regional variation, overall levels of illiteracy (a standard measure of the development of any society) fell rapidly, from 53 per cent in 1841 to 18 per cent in 1891. Irish children enjoyed the benefits of a standardised syllabus and the attentions of inspectors, whose task was to ensure that standards were kept throughout the country.

Although disused, the building remains in good repair and is enhanced by the retention of its historic slate roof, cast-iron gutters and drainpipes, timber sash windows and doors. In addition to the architectural interest of the building, this small school was of undoubtedly great social importance to the local community.

DESERTED SCHOOLHOUSES OF IRELAND

Drumlish National School

Drumlish townland, County Longford (dated c. 1930)

Drumlish in north County Longford is close to the border with Cavan and Leitrim. Just outside the centre of the village is Old School Road where a series of old schoolhouses have stood over the past 180 years. The first edition Ordnance Survey map from the mid-nineteenth century shows a schoolhouse marked at the southern side of the modern R198 where the Cairn Hill View estate is now located. However, the school featured here is of a later date and is located to the east of the School Road junction on the southern side of Old School Road.

Layers of colourful paint peel from the walls of the classroom.

A solitary chair remains in the classroom.

Here, hidden behind trees and brambles, are the remains of a detached, seven-bay, single-storey, former H-plan primary school, originally constructed *c.* 1930 and extended *c.* 1950.

Standing beside the building is a pebble-dashed water tower typical of 1950s school construction, while to the rear is a concrete playground shelter, which was cast *in situ*. It is a particularly evocative abandoned schoolhouse, only going out of use in recent years. On entering the school through either of the cold, cast-*in-situ* side entrances, its functional 1950s architecture gives the interior a haunting feel, as encroaching nature gradually reclaims the building.

Although now derelict, this former school building retains much of its fabric and its overall structure. Its present form is the result of the combination of a H-plan block, with typical tall windows and high ceilings, with later, frankly modern, cloakroom extensions.

The classrooms are in various states of decay. In the older 1930s section, the peeling plasterwork reveals an almost hypnotic brick construction underneath.

The original symmetrical construction is typical of the standard school buildings designed and built in great numbers by the OPW for the Board of Education during the first decades of independence. The six-room schoolhouse indicates that there was a large young population in the Drumlish area in the early twentieth century.

The separate entrances for boys and girls, and the division of the playgrounds and the play shelter, would have been typical of the separation of the sexes in rural schools during the first half of the twentieth century. This interesting and quite complex school building is an integral part of the built and social heritage of the local area.

Graffiti on the schoolyard shelter.

Pastel colours
through
doorways.

The art deco entrance.

The haunting hallway is now silent.

Water gathers in the hall below a hole in the ceiling.

The stalls in the modern bathroom to the rear of the school.

St Joseph's National School

Leitir, Islandeady, County Mayo (dated late nineteenth century)

About halfway along the road from Westport to Castlebar there is a boggy rural spot hidden amongst the drumlins called Islandeady. It still has four (small) working national schools: Cloggernagh, Cornanool, Cougala and Leitir. But the schoolhouse at Leitir replaced an earlier school building that still stands, and it is this structure that features here. Today its modern successor has just six girls and four boys on the coming year's enrolment, and one wonders if it is likely to stay open for much longer.

A crumbling classroom.

Now-redundant school desks are stacked against the back wall.

The original schoolhouse at Leitir is on a low rise over a small local road just a few hundred metres from its successor. In form, the old Leitir schoolhouse is identical to the one at Ballymackeehola (also in County Mayo), which dates to 1895, and though there is no date plaque at Leitir, it is probably of a similar date.

Leitir is a two-room schoolhouse. The building comprises a detached, four-bay, single-storey national school with a pitched slate roof. Like Ballymackeehola, the interior of the schoolhouse remains in a good state of preservation with many of the original fittings and fixtures still in place. Even more remarkable, though, is the fact that much of the original school furniture is still scattered around the building. Each of the classrooms also contains a brickwork open fireplace that is typical of these old school buildings.

The main classroom, now dark and lifeless.

Inishkea (South) Island National School

Inishkea South, County Mayo (dated c. 1900)

Getting to the Inishkea Islands off the west coast of County Mayo can be difficult. There is no ferry service or regular connection between the mainland and the two islands. Located out beyond Blacksod Bay, the islands have been uninhabited since 1934, apart from flocks of free-roaming sheep and a thriving seal colony. The islands are about 45 minutes out to sea, passing the scenic coastline of Achill on glistening silver waves.

The entrance to the old schoolhouse.

The interior, with almost all or the features eroded by the weather.

The Inishkea Islands have lain almost untouched since the last permanent residents left. Visitors are infrequent by all accounts, though a man has reportedly been living on the north island for two years without contact, electricity or even a boat.

Pulling into 'the anchorage' at Porteenbeg on the sheltered eastern side of the island, you pass the diminutive Rusheen Island where there are the remains of an old whaling station. Ahead on the shore is a line of crumbling stone houses overlooking a white deserted beach. The sea is clear and turquoise, calm and sheltered on the eastern side of the island, even though waves can be seen crashing silently on the western shore in the distance, that coastline being exposed to the Atlantic.

The story of the Inishkea Islands and how they came to be abandoned in 1934 is a sad one. The islands supported a population for thousands of years. The earliest evidence of settlement dates back at least 5,000 years and there are numerous archaeological sites from the Neolithic period and several Early

The weather-beaten remains of
the school near the shore.

A view from the school window toward the mainland.

Christian monastic sites. In 1946, the French archaeologist Françoise Henry excavated evidence of a seventh-century dye workshop on Inishkea North where monks were producing dye from the shells of the dog whelk. But in more recent centuries, people were primarily engaged in fishing and farming. The population was enough to support schoolhouses on both the north and the south islands.

However, on 28 October 1927, the men from the islands were night-fishing in the clear waters surround the islands when a sudden, violent storm blew up, which caught them unawares. Some of the currachs managed to reach home but several failed to return. One reputedly was taken all the way to the mainland, where it fetched up with its crew unharmed. In the morning, it was discovered that several currachs and ten young fishermen had been lost. The island community was devastated and never fully recovered from the tragedy. By 1934 most of the inhabitants had been voluntarily rehoused at Glosh and Faulmore on the Mullet Peninsula. At that time, the national school at Aughlem on the mainland was extended to accommodate the resettled island children but it signalled the demise of traditional life on the island. The old schoolhouses on Inishkea North and South were left to fall apart.

The schoolhouse is made of local granite stone. Today it is but a shell and nearly nine decades of exposure to the Atlantic have taken their toll. There is no roof, there are no remaining distinguishing features, the fireplace in the gable wall has been robbed, and if there was ever a name and date plaque, it is gone, too.

In form, it is very similar to the example on nearby Achill Beg Island (see page 174); the rubble-and-brick construction comprises a detached, single-storey, two-bay, one-room schoolhouse with a tall, single-light window at its northern gable. The schoolhouse at Achill Beg dates to 1903, and this schoolhouse is likely to be of a similar date.

Achill Beg National School

Achill Beg Island, County Mayo (dated 1903)

If you were to include just about every rocky outcrop of notable size, then you could count at least 500 or so islands off the coast of Ireland. However, only a handful of these islands have maintained a population through history, and even fewer still have retained permanent residents to the present day. Through the Early and High Medieval period many of the smaller islands off the west coast attracted monastic settlers. Off the west coast, monastic settlements can be found on Skellig Michael, St Macdara's Island, Scattery Island and Inishmurray, to name but a few, with the early monks being drawn to the isolation offered by these punishing outposts.

The exposed stone and-mortar structure of the worn-out old school building.

The view from the window of the only classroom.

However, our interest is in the nineteenth and twentieth centuries and the experiences of those who lived and were educated on these islands at that time. Examining the early mapping sources, like the first edition 6-inch map (1829–1842) and first edition 25-inch map (1897–1913), it can be seen that up until the mid-twentieth century there were some 40 national schools on Irish islands. Life on many of these islands could be harsh at the best of times and by the 1950s residents of many of the smaller islands were encouraged to leave and settle on the mainland. As a consequence of this 'evacuation', the majority of the 40 island national schools were closed. Some have unfortunately been completely destroyed by the elements, such as the schoolhouse once located on the eastern shore of Scattery Island, County Clare. Others have been restored as holiday homes, for example on Dursey Island, County Cork. And some, such as the example featured here from Achill Beg, have been sitting vacant and abandoned since the island was evacuated in the mid-twentieth century.

Achill Beg is just south of Achill Island off the Corraun Peninsula in County

Roofless and weather-beaten by the wild Atlantic.

Mayo. The topography comprises two low, rocky hills with a shallow valley between. The island covers just 60 hectares and is separated from the rest of Achill by a narrow channel, the Blind Sound. Access to the island is from Cé Mhór, in the village of An Chloich Mhór (Cloghmore), by local arrangement.

Nobody lives on Achill Beg any more. Before the Great Famine of the 1840s, its population was just under 200 people, but by the early 1960s it had decreased to just six. In 1965 Achill Beg was evacuated and the inhabitants were settled on Achill and the nearby mainland. Nowadays, a handful of cottages have been restored as holiday homes, although there are no permanent residents. During the nineteenth and twentieth centuries, settlement was primarily on the east of the island and in the saddle between the two low hills. It is in this saddle that you can find the remains of the island's old school

The rubble-and-brick construction comprises a detached, single-storey, three-bay, one-room schoolhouse. Although very similar in form to the example from Sonnagh Old in County Galway (see page 121), the schoolhouse on Achill Beg includes a tall, single-light window at its western gable, which affords a spectacular view from the fireplace located at the opposing eastern gable.

Time and the elements have most certainly taken their toll on the building, and all that remains today is the walling: the roof has collapsed and the bare remains stand as a simple tribute to the former population of the now deserted island. Inside, the wainscoting has largely been peeled from the walls and the floor has completely rotted. It is a cold and sorry sight.

The brickwork and cut-stone fireplace remains in situ.

Paddy Kilbane was born on Achill Beg and educated in the schoolhouse during the 1950s. He relates how the fate of Achill Beg was sealed in the 1950s when electricity was brought to the locality, but not to the island. The islanders relied on oil lamps for light, and rechargeable batteries for the island's one wireless set. They grew tired of the hardship, and one family after the next took their opportunity to leave and settle elsewhere; some settled on the mainland, some emigrated, never to return. Paddy himself spent his younger years in London but recounted tales of going to local dances on the mainland in his teens. When the weather was rough and he and his friends could not row back to the island after their night out, they would sleep in cowsheds until the weather improved.

Paddy also had fond memories of the school and the final schoolteacher there, a 21-year-old woman named Breege Henry. By 1959, she taught just ten pupils at the school, all with the surname Gallagher, all brothers and sisters. Ms Henry had been preceded by a Mr MacNamara in the 1940s. Paddy believed him to be ahead of his time when he took it upon himself to use the school building as a night school for the adult islanders, teaching many of them to read and write.

It is clear from listening to Paddy that the schoolhouse on Achill Beg was a focal point of life on the island. Now, with the former population aging and dispersed, it seems especially poignant to see the building wither and decay.

Shanvaghera National School

Shanvaghera, County Mayo (dated 1935)

Shanvaghera National School is situated in the townland of the same name, just off the N17, a few kilometres north of Knock in County Mayo. Although the exterior of the building is not particularly striking, the interior is well preserved. The building is certainly in a ruinous state, with nature invading through the shattered glass and broken doorways. Nonetheless, original features such as the wooden partition that divided the main room into three classrooms, three original fireplaces, and a single school desk add wonderful atmosphere to this building. The separate entrances for boys and girls are to the rear of the school,

Looking into the classroom.

The long narrow classroom in morning light.

Old bicycles in the hallway.

A stove is set into the original fireplace.

and the numbered coat hooks once used by the pupils can be seen in the entrance hall. The suspended wooden floor was solid enough to walk on when I visited. The school closed in 1968/69.

To the rear of the main building is the former toilet block where the wooden elements of the non-flushing latrines remain.

The building comprises a detached, five-bay, single-storey national school, built and opened in 1935, on a T-shaped plan with single-bay, single-storey, lean-to projecting bays centred on single-bay, full-height, gabled projecting porch; there is a seven-bay, single-storey rear (east) elevation. The school retains its pitched slate roof, which extends over the lean-to projecting bays. It has lichen-covered chimney stacks with chamfered capping supporting terracotta pots and cast-iron 'rainwater goods' (i.e. drainpipes and gutters). The window openings are square-headed with cut-limestone sills and concealed dressings framing the remains of six-over-six timber sash windows centred on four-over-four timber sash windows with six-over-six timber sash windows to rear (east) elevation.

There are square-headed opposing door openings with concealed dressings framing timber boarded or tongue-and-groove timber panelled doors.

This is a dilapidated national school erected to a standardised design for the Department of Education, representing an integral component of the twentieth-century architectural heritage of County Mayo. A prolonged period of neglect notwithstanding, the elementary form and massing survive intact together with substantial quantities of the original fabric, thus upholding much of the character of a national school. It makes a forlorn visual statement in a rural street scene.

The second edition Ordnance Survey sheet for the area, which dates to the closing years of the nineteenth century, shows that there was a school on this site before 1935, and in all likelihood the present building represents a renovated schoolhouse dating originally to the late nineteenth or early twentieth century.

Corvoy National School

Cornahoe townland, County Monaghan (dated c. 1902)

During the closing decades of the nineteenth century, there was a notable increase in the construction of new schoolhouses in Ireland. A number of 'to-plan' designs were utilised across the country, including the detached, eight-bay, single-storey schoolhouse, like the example featured here from Corvoy in County Monaghan, built in 1902, and at Carrigan County Cavan, built in 1897 (see page 55).

Corvoy National School replaced a mid-nineteenth-century school building to the west, close to the Roman Catholic Church of the Holy Rosary. The form and layout of Corvoy National School is typical of an early-twentieth century

A piano remains in the bare, white classroom.

rural Irish national school, many of which were built at this time to the standard designs supplied by the OPW. The plan accommodated two classrooms and cloakrooms, for boys and girls, within a symmetrical building. A dividing wall separated the sexes to the east, and a lean-to outbuilding acted as a lavatory. The character of the school is intact, with original timber casement windows. The school is of architectural and social significance, its social and central role in the community enhanced by the presence of a post-Independence letterbox included in the school boundary wall, a notable example of the high quality of mass-produced cast-ironwork produced in Ireland in the early twentieth century.

The school has a pitched slate roof with single red-brick chimney stack to mid-roof, and cast-iron 'rainwater goods' (i.e. drainpipes and gutters). There is a carved stone date plaque to the centre of the front (west) elevation.

Inside, it is whitewashed and bare, bright but empty. It retains the majority of its original features, including a built-in cloak cupboard inside the northern doorway. The school remains in good condition both internally and externally and so it is a fine example of this 'to-standard' design.

Detail of the doorway into the classroom.

Latton National School

Latton townland, County Monaghan (dated c. 1941)

In the village of Latton in County Monaghan there has been a progression of four schoolhouses since the first school building was marked on the first edition Ordnance Survey map in 1829–1842. The national school featured here dates to 1941, and was replaced by the modern school building situated closer to the centre of the village. Broadly similar in form and fabric to the school at Gortadooda in County Tipperary, this was a standard design by the Board of Works that was used throughout the country in the late 1930s and early 1940s. Now standing in

Looking out the classroom doorway to the hall.

open pasture, the structure is gradually giving way to the elements. To the front of the building there is an inscribed limestone date and name plaque reading 'Scoil Mhuire Leacht Fhinn Scoil Náisiúnta 1941'. Inside, many of the fixtures and fittings remain, and each classroom retains much of the original furniture, giving the environment a particularly eerie feeling.

Although in poor condition, it retains its form, scale and much of the original fabric, and is a reminder of the network of small primary schools provided throughout rural Ireland in the early twentieth century, and of the social importance of improving access to education.

Furniture thrown to the corner of the classroom, beneath an air vent.

DESERTED SCHOOLHOUSES OF IRELAND

Broken desks scattered across the classroom.

Detail of the light switch.

The blackboard still hangs on the wall.

Bunnanadden National School

Ballynaraw South, County Sligo (dated 1883)

County Sligo in the north-west of Ireland is undoubtedly rich in history, heritage, mythology and folklore. The dramatic and spectacular landscape rises from the wild Atlantic coast with expansive, sandy dunes and beaches, to the Tolkien-esque Dartry Mountains where every cave, cliff face and hill has its own unique story to tell.

This environment lends itself easily to storytelling and the imagination, and it is easy to see why it has inspired and featured in a wealth of fantastical folklore throughout the millennia.

An external view of Bunnanadden School.

A sheep peeks through the classroom door.

Bedding for livestock strewn across the classroom floor.

The original cupboards within the classroom.

Within the rolling hills of the drumlin belt in south County Sligo, and under the shadow of the Bricklieve Mountains, is the sleepy hamlet of Bunnanadden (Bunnanaddan or Bunninadden), 9km from Tubbercurry and 8km from Ballymote.

During the late nineteenth century this was a busy spot with a local mill, two churches, a constabulary barracks and a sylvan street scene with a row of detached houses. On a low rise to the north-east of the village was the local schoolhouse overlooking the goings-on below.

DESERTED SCHOOLHOUSES OF IRELAND

A plaque on the northern end of the building dates its construction to 1883 although the first edition Ordnance Survey sheet shows that there was a pre-existing school at this site in at least the 1840s. Although in ruin, the interior is relatively well preserved, with the brightly painted walls having a now ghostly patina.

The building is of a standard design, comprising a detached, multi-bay, single-storey, rendered construction. It has two contiguous three-bay, north–south classroom blocks with gabled entrance porches to north end of the east and west elevations.

The pitched roof is feeling the strain of time but it still protects the interior from the elements. When I visited the school in March 2016, the building was home to two inquisitive and woolly schoolchildren.

This traditional village school retains most of its original features and, although derelict, is a good example of an unaltered late-nineteenth-century national school, with large well-proportioned classrooms and clear segregation of accommodation for male and female pupils.

Drumatemple National School

Drumatemple, County Roscommon (dated 1935)

Situated about a kilometre outside the County Galway village of Ballymoe but just across the county border in Roscommon, Drumatemple National School stands near the N60 roadside. A plaque next to the door dates this two-room, detached, single-storey schoolhouse to 1935, although the second edition Ordnance Survey sheet shows that there was a school building at this location at the turn of the twentieth century.

The schoolhouse is boarded-up and today used for storage. However, it is in a relatively good state of preservation with much of the interior still surviving and much of the original furniture still present. The record of 'pupils on roll in the ordinary national schools of County Roscommon in the year 1890' shows that this was a busy schoolhouse – with the sizeable attendance of 172 – most likely servicing the nearby village of Ballymoe.

With the windows heavily boarded-up and the rooms in total darkness, only a handful of long-exposure photographs managed to reveal the interior of the building. Painted in bright blue and yellow, it is clear that this building has not changed much since its construction in 1935.

Sunlight lances through the boarded-up windows in the only accessible classroom in the building.

Looking along the dark corridor.

Notes

1 Coolahan, J. (1981) *'Irish Education: Its History and Structure'* Institute of Public Administration, Dublin.

2 Young, Arthur. (1780) *A Tour in Ireland 1776–1779.* 2 Vols. Dublin, p. 107.

3 Corcoran, T. (1928) *Selected Texts on Education Systems in Ireland from the Close of the Middle Ages.* Dublin: UCD, p. 62.

4 Keenan, D. (2006) *Post-Famine Ireland: Social Structure: Ireland as it really was.* Xlibris Corporation.

5 Fernández-Suárez, Y. (2006) 'An Essential Picture in a Sketch-Book of Ireland: The Last Hedge Schools.' In *Estudios Irlandeses*, Number 1. Almería.

6 Coolahan, *op. cit.*, p. 6.

7 Keenan, D., *op. cit.*, pp 383–4.

8 Hyland, Á. & Milne, K. eds. (1987) *Irish Educational Documents.* Vol I (A Selection of Extracts from Documents Relating to the History of Irish Education from the Earliest Times to 1922). Dublin: CICE, p. 116.

9 Coolahan, *op. cit.*, p. 8.

10 Keenan, *op. cit.*, p. 88.

11 Coolahan, J. Kilfeather, F, and Hussey, C. (2012) *'The Forum on Patronage and Pluralism in the Primary Sector'* Unpublished Report of the Forum's Advisory Group.

12 Central Statistics Office: www.cso.ie/en/media/csoie/releasespublications/documents/statisticalyear book/2012/c1population.pdf

13 *Ibid.*

14 The Congested Districts comprised all or parts of the counties of: Donegal. Sligo, Monaghan, Cavan, Longford, Leitrim, Mayo, Galway, Offaly, Clare, Tipperary, Limerick, Cork and Kerry. It is these areas which today contain the greatest numbers of abandoned schoolhouses.

15 Glassie, H. (2000) *Vernacular Architecture*, Indiana University Press, p. 22.

16 *Ibid.*

17 *Ibid.*

18 Rynne, C. (2006) *Industrial Ireland 1750–1930*, The Collins Press, Cork, p. 317.

19 See for example: Bernard 1848, Patterson 1875 and Shawkey 1910.

20 'The NIAH includes in its surveys a broad range of structures and sites covering the period from 1700 to the present day. These include structures of simple design and function, such as post boxes and waterpumps, to grand architectural statements including cathedrals and country houses … NIAH surveys are not comprehensive and there are sites of importance that may have been missed.' (NIAH 2017). www.buildingsofireland.ie/FindOutMore/Frequently%20Asked%20Questions%20 (15.09.2017).pdf

21 Coolahan, *op. cit.* (1981), p. 6.

22 Upitis, R. (2004) School Architecture and Complexity in *Complicity: An International Journal of Complexity and Education Volume 1, Number 1*, p. 20.

23 De Silva, S. (2014) 'Beyond Ruin Porn: What's Behind Our Obsession with Decay?' Online article, available at: www.archdaily.com/author/shayari-de-silva (accessed 12 December 2017).

24 Delle, J. A. (1998) '*An Archaeology of Social Space: Analysing Coffee Plantations in Jamaica's Blue Mountains*', Plenum Press, New York, p. 37.

25 Holtorf, C. and Williams, H. (2001) 'Landscapes and Memories' in *Historical Archaeology*. Hicks, D. and Beaudry, M.C. (eds) Cambridge University Press, Cambridge, p. 235.

26 Tilley, C. (1994) '*Places, Paths and Monuments; A Phenomenology of Landscape*', Berg Publishers, Oxford, p. 17.

27 Holtorf and Williams, *op. cit.*

28 *Ibid.*

29 Walsh, T. (2004). 'A Historical Overview of Our Conceptualisation of Childhood in Ireland in the Twentieth Century'. A presentation by Thomas Walsh, Development Officer (CECDE) at the Human Development Conference, 'Voices and Images of Childhood and Adolescence: Rethinking Young People's Identities', 16 October 2004.

30 Mydland, L. (2011) 'The legacy of one-room schoolhouses: A comparative study of the American Midwest and Norway' In *European Journal of American Studies Vol. 6 No 1.*

31 Keenan, (2006) *op. cit.* p. 86.

32 *Ibid.*

33 Keenan, D. (2016) *The Social History of Ireland: Including the Seamy Side*, Xlibris Corporation, p. 45.

34 Lynch, K. (2004). *Equality and Power in Schools: Redistribution, Recognition and Representation.* Psychology Press Routledge, London, p. 84.

35 *Ibid.*, p. 85.

36 Rynne, *op. cit.*, p. 317.

37 *Ibid.*, p. 315.

38 Chambers, J. 'Islands – Change in Population 1841–2011'. Available at http://irishislands.info/census/graphs/numbers.html

Bibliography

Anon. (1846). *The Sessional Papers of The House of Lords 1846 Vol. XXXVI.* London

Avery, D. (2003). *Victorian and Edwardian Architecture.* Chaucer Press Books, Oxford.

Bernard, H. (1848). *School Architecture, or, Contributions to the Improvement of School-houses in the United States.* H.W. Derby, Cincinnati.

Coolahan, J. (1973). 'A Study of Curricular Policy for the Primary and Secondary Schools of Ireland 1900–1935, with Special Reference to the Irish Language and Irish History.' PHD thesis, Trinity College Dublin

Coolahan, J. (1981). *Irish Education: Its History and Structure.* Institute of Public Administration, Dublin

Coolahan, J. Kilfeather, F, and Hussey, C. (2012). 'The Forum on Patronage and Pluralism in the Primary Sector'. Unpublished report of the forum's advisory group, Dublin.

Corcoran, T. (1928). *Selected Texts on Education Systems in Ireland from the Close of the Middle Ages.* University College Dublin, Dublin

Delle, J. A. (1998). '*An Archaeology of Social Space: Analysing Coffee Plantations in Jamaica's Blue Mountains',* Plenum Press, New York.

DCMS (2010). '*Principles of Selection for Listing Buildings*' Public Document of the Department of Culture, Media and Sport, Available at: www.gov.uk/government/publications/principles-of-selection-for-listing-buildings. Accessed 15 December 2017

De Silva, S. (2014). 'Beyond Ruin Porn: What's Behind Our Obsession with Decay?' Online article, available at: www.archdaily.com/author/shayari-de-silva

Dudek, M. (2008). '*Architecture of Schools: The New Learning Environments*' Architectural Press, New York.

Eveleth, S.F. (1978). *Victorian School-house Architecture: A Facsimile of Samuel F. Eveleth's School-house Architecture, a Pattern Book of 1870.* American Life Foundation, New York

Fernández-Suárez, Y. (2006). 'An Essential Picture in a Sketch-Book of Ireland: The Last Hedge Schools'. In *Estudios Irlandeses,* No 1, Almería

Gargano, E. (2008). *Reading Victorian Schoolrooms: Childhood and Education in Nineteenth-Century Fiction.* Routledge, New York

Glassie, H. (2000). *Vernacular Architecture.* Indiana University Press, USA

Historic England (2017). Online article, available at: historicengland.org.uk/advice/hpg/hpr-definitions/. Accessed 17 December 2017

Holtorf, C. and Williams, H. (2001). 'Landscapes and Memories' in *Historical Archaeology.* Hicks, D. and Beaudry, M.C. (eds). Cambridge University Press, Cambridge.

Hyland, Á. & Milne, K. (eds). (1987*). Irish Educational Documents.* Vol I (A Selection of Extracts from Documents Relating to the History of Irish Education from the Earliest Times to 1922). CICE, Dublin

Keenan, D. (2006). *Post-Famine Ireland: Social Structure: Ireland As It Really Was.* Xlibris Corporation, Dublin

Keenan, D. (2016). *The Social History of Ireland: Including the Seamy Side.* Xlibris Corporation, Dublin

Lynch, K. (2004). *Equality and Power in Schools: Redistribution, Recognition and Representation.* Psychology Press Routledge, London

McManus, A. (2014). *Irish Education; The Ministerial Legacy, 1919–99.* The History Press, Dublin

Mydland, L. (2011). 'The legacy of one-room schoolhouses: A comparative study of the American Midwest and Norway' In *European Journal of American Studies Vol. 6 No 1*

NIAH (2017). 'Frequently Asked Questions'. Public Document of the National Inventory of Architectural Heritage. Available at: www.buildingsofireland. ie/FindOutMore/Frequently%20Asked%20Questions%20(15.09.2017).pdf. Accessed 17 December 2017

Patterson, W.M. (1875). '*A Manual of Architecture for Churches, Parsonages and School-houses Containing Designs, Elevations, Plans, Specifications*', Methodist Episcopal Church, Nashville

Rynne, C. (2006). *Industrial Ireland 1750–1930,* The Collins Press, Cork

Tilley, C. (1994). '*Places, Paths and Monuments; A Phenomenology of Landscape*', Berg Publishers, Oxford

Shawkey, M.P. (1910). *School Architecture – Containing Articles and Illustrations on School Grounds, Houses, Out-Buildings, Heating, Ventilation, School Decoration, Furniture, And Fixtures.* The News-mail, Charleston

Walsh, T. (2014). 'A Historical Overview Of Our Conceptualisation Of Childhood In Ireland In The Twentieth Century'. A presentation by Thomas Walsh, Development Officer (CECDE) at the Human Development Conference, 'Voices and Images of Childhood and Adolescence: Rethinking Young People's Identities', 16 October 2004

Weiner, D.E.B. (1994). *Architecture and Social Reform in Late-Victorian London.* Manchester University Press, Manchester.

Upitis, R. (2004). 'School Architecture and Complexity' in *Complicity: An International Journal of Complexity and Education Vol. 1, No 1.* Alberta

Young, Arthur. 1780. *A Tour in Ireland 1776–1779.* 2 vols. George Bell and Sons, London.